Women, Power,
Politics

Women, Power,
Politics

The Hidden Story of Canada's
Unfinished Democracy

Sylvia Bashevkin

OXFORD
UNIVERSITY PRESS

OXFORD
UNIVERSITY PRESS

70 Wynford Drive, Don Mills, Ontario M3C 1J9
www.oupcanada.com

Oxford University Press is a department of the University of Oxford.
It furthers the University's objective of excellence in research, scholarship,
and education by publishing worldwide in

Oxford   New York

Auckland Cape Town Dar es Salaam Hong Kong Karachi Kuala Lumpur Madrid
Melbourne Mexico City Nairobi New Delhi Shanghai Taipei Toronto

With offices in

Argentina Austria Brazil Chile Czech Republic France Greece
Guatemala Hungary Italy Japan Poland Portugal SingaporeSouth Korea
Switzerland Thailand Turkey Ukraine Vietnam

Oxford is a trade mark of Oxford University Press in the UK and in certain other countries

Published in Canada by Oxford University Press

Library and Archives Canada Cataloguing in Publication

Bashevkin, Sylvia B
Women, power, politics : the hidden story of Canada's
unfinished democracy / Sylvia Bashevkin.

Includes bibliographical references and index.
ISBN 978-0-19-543170-4

1. Women in politics—Canada. 2. Women
politicians—Canada. 3. Representative government
and representation—Canada. I. Title.
HQ1236.5.C2B37 2009   320.082'0971   C2008-907102-6

Cover image: Sheila Copps. Photo by Donald Weber/Getty Images

1 2 3 4 – 12 11 10 09

Oxford University Press is committed to our environment. This book is printed on Forest
Stewardship Council certified paper which contains 100% post-consumer waste.

For D.M.B.L. and A.D.B.L.

Table of Contents

Preface

I wrote most of this manuscript during the summer and fall of 2007, when the excitement and, indeed, euphoria over what looked like the imminent nomination of Hillary Rodham Clinton as the Democratic candidate for president of the United States was at its peak. Commentators pronounced and, in some cases, celebrated her role as the unbeatable front-runner, the woman who would make history not only by securing the nomination, but also by winning the fall 2008 election and becoming America's first ever female president. If any confusion or doubt surrounded this hullabaloo, it seemed to apply only to the question of how Senator Clinton's husband, former US President Bill Clinton, would adjust to life as the number two person in the White House. Could he become a decorous "First Guy," much like the proverbial First Lady of American public life? Would the couple be known as President and Mr. Clinton?

Relative to this surge of confident optimism vis-à-vis American politics, prospects for women in Canada looked bleak or, at best, stalemated. True to form, we began to analyze ourselves in light of the continental comparison. Were our parliamentary institutions blocking the wider opportunities that had seemingly accrued to women in the American congressional system? Did stronger individualist norms in the US create proportionately more ambitious, motivated women candidates? How did voters there manage to demand more gender-balanced political elites? Simply stated, what was wrong north of the 49th parallel?

Frankly, I was never convinced that Hillary Clinton's path to the White House was quite as smoothly paved as the early reports suggested. Even a cursory glance at legislative figures shows that the percentages of women in the US House of Representatives during recent decades have generally been below those in the Canadian House of Commons. Neither country comes close to approaching levels in the Nordic countries—for example, women's numerical representation in elective office south of the 49th parallel has been especially weak and has arguably plateaued during recent years.

In fact, had Clinton and her team chosen to study the matter, they could have learned a great deal from the experiences of women in Canadian politics, particularly those who have sought senior leadership roles in our political parties. Developments in Canada since the mid-1970s demonstrate that women seeking top posts in elective office frequently have their leadership styles, personal attributes such as clothing and age, not to mention personal lives, dissected in full public view.

The upshot of these grueling evaluations is often a sense that Woman X falls short on each and every metric. Yet Hillary Clinton's own handlers seemed genuinely stunned that their candidate was hit by contradictory accusations that she was somehow too tough and too soft, too well-dressed and too frumpy, too old and too inexperienced. Above all, they looked flummoxed in the face of powerful charges that Senator Clinton was married to a man who was either too outspoken and interfering, or else too feeble and outdated, to be helpful to her campaign.

Judging by the pattern by which women have only won top posts in relatively weak federal parties in Canada, it's fair to suggest that Clinton's chances at securing the Democratic nomination would have been significantly better in 2004 than in 2008. This is not to suggest that she should not have run when she did, or that the problems in her 2008 campaign were insurmountable. Rather, the core premise of this book is that we as Canadians have much to learn from our own experiences. Similarly, citizens of other democracies can also draw useful lessons from what happened here.

The chapters that follow uncover a visceral discomfort with women and power, which comes to the surface especially clearly in competitive political environments. In these contexts, the traditional equation of men with leadership asserts itself in such a way as to profoundly disadvantage female politicians. Like many Canadian women whose careers in public office are discussed in detail in this study, Hillary Clinton confronted the multiple real-world manifestations of a social unease that's hard to touch, but remains compelling and influential nevertheless. To her credit, she persevered in the face of considerable odds against her nomination, and did not waver in her commitment to mounting a serious, energetic, and issue-based campaign.

The premise of *Women, Power, Politics* is not that gender constitutes the sole over-arching barrier facing either Hillary Clinton or her Canadian counterparts. Instead, our discussion is grounded in a realization that electoral politics is a rough-and-tumble blood sport, one in which many talented, highly qualified individuals falter in the course of their careers in public service for reasons that have little to do with their ability to serve the public. We need to think longer and harder about how to attract more good people to democratic politics, and how to treat with a greater degree of fairness those who are willing to take the plunge.

For their willingness to support me in the course of writing this book, I thank my literary lawyer, Marian Hebb, who has long insisted that it was a project worth undertaking. Jennie Rubio, my editor at Oxford University Press, was consistently enthusiastic and encouraging. Professor Miriam Smith of York University kindly undertook a thorough review of the full manuscript, and pushed me forward through the last round of revisions. Since the early 1980s, my undergraduate and graduate students in political science at the University of Toronto have shed new light on questions raised in this field. With the generous support of the Social Sciences and Humanities Research Council of Canada, I was able to attend party conventions, meet large numbers of female politicians and think about the challenges facing women in politics in broad international terms. The bold candour of the activists I met has been inspiring; I genuinely appreciate their openness and honesty, and remain in their debt.

Above all, I am most grateful to my daughters for their optimism about our ability to create a better, more equal world. In recognition of their love and hope, this book is dedicated to both of them.

~ 1 ~

Introduction

What image does the phrase "women on top" evoke in your mind? Is it a sultry scene of a sexually aroused, well-sculpted woman atop an excited man with a smile on his face? Or—if you are middle-aged or older—perhaps your mind recalls the slim, leggy model of the 1970s, perched on a carton of Virginia Slims cigarettes beneath that famous tagline, "You've come a long way, baby."

Whichever variation on those visual themes pops into view, odds are the first scene you imagined was not a female prime minister or premier speaking forcefully or listening attentively at the cabinet table, or Madam Mayor engaged in intense debate with her colleagues on city council. In fact, this book probes what I have come to understand, after decades of research in the field, as a profound disconnect between our conceptualizations of women and power.

The study identifies the origins of that gap in a deep-seated psychological discomfort we have with accepting women and political authority together, in the same picture frame or equation. As in many parts of the democratic world, we in Canada tend to carry around gender "schemas" or frameworks—sometimes subtle, and often bluntly obvious—that limit the ability of women to contribute to public life. These schemas are reflected in the tendencies of journalists, other politicians, and each of us as citizens to dissect *ad infinitum* the ways in which women in high office demonstrate their leadership abilities, select what to wear, express ideas, and even organize their romantic lives. Not surprisingly, at the culmination of the dissection process, judgments usually pronounce as deficient those few women who reach the top of the political heap.

In Canada, we have developed a peculiar but highly virulent strain of this *women plus power equals discomfort* syndrome—also referred to here as the *discomfort equation*. Our homegrown version directly associates female political elites with bad-news election results. How did this happen? In a nutshell, the ability of women to win elite positions in parties that were not in a competitive position vis-à-vis government power was taken as a blueprint for failure once those women-led parties did what logic predicted—they remained in an uncompetitive position.

Unlike men who lead marginal parties to marginal results, women who lead weak parties to weak results have frequently been grouped together on the basis of their gender. As a result, not only do we have general jitters about women in top public posts, but also we draw specific conclusions on the basis of a few women who rose to top positions and whose parties then fared poorly at the ballot box. The Canadian version of the *discomfort equation* thus carries with it a visceral unease about loss, defeat, and even humiliation.

Permit me to cut directly to the chase. This argument is explicitly *not* a male conspiracy theory. As the evidence presented in this and the following chapters demonstrates, women have contributed to, and can help to fix, the problems facing female politicians. After all, as citizens, we share a collective responsibility for improving the quality of our polity. Toward that end, the final chapter of this book proposes a series of reforms for people of both genders to pursue, which together can enhance our comfort levels with women in public life, and thereby strengthen the fabric of Canadian democracy.

"Whoa, hold your horses," an insightful reader might interject at this very early stage in our conversation. "Your starting premise is simply not correct. Aren't about 20 percent of our members of Parliament women right now? We've had women premiers in at least two provinces, plus a female prime minister, however briefly, in 1993. Women have led political parties across this country. Record numbers of young women are currently enrolled in our post-secondary institutions, completing undergraduate programs plus pursuing law and business degrees to an unprecedented extent. And just because the phrase 'women on top' fails to evoke political images right away does not, by itself, constitute proof there's a representational problem."

I agree. Each of these observations about MPs, premiers, Prime Minister Kim Campbell, party leaders, university enrolments, and visual images is empirically correct. None, however, provides the necessary underpinning for a compelling counter-argument, which would assert we're on a smooth path to political nirvana because women are steadily gaining ground in Canadian public life. Although I'm by nature optimistic, I believe the view that things are moving along nicely is flat-out wrong.

Moreover, rather than experiencing smooth forward motion, women's political status in Canada is arguably on a rocky path, and likely jolting backward in reverse gear. Boldly stated, the prospects for Canadian women who seek careers in public life seem to be getting worse, not better. The most hopeful assessment I can offer (as someone who always tries to find the silver lining in every cloud) is that we're facing a stagnation or plateau that could, if we act promptly and effectively, serve as the launching pad for progress down the road, hopefully in the not-too-distant future.

For many years, we've conveniently assumed that advances in other sectors—notably in formal education, the paid workforce, constitutional equality rights in the Canadian Charter of Rights and Freedoms, and so on— meant women's political advancement would inevitably march right along as well. Yet compelling evidence to the contrary has accumulated right beneath our blinkered eyes.

Since hindsight offers near-perfect vision, let's peer briefly into the rearview mirror. Looking far back to the immediate postwar decades, we see a House of Commons and provincial legislatures with tiny fractions of women members, and perhaps one woman at a time in cabinet. The second-wave feminist mobilization of the late 1960s and following helped to boost these numbers dramatically, to the point that our federal Parliament went from four female MPs in 1967 to 65 in 2008. Numbers at the sub-national level also increased to the point that women presently hold about 22 percent of provincial seats, up from roughly 6 percent during the early 1980s.

Since the heady days of the 1970s and 1980s, however, we've mostly seen stagnation. The proportion of female MPs has been stuck in the roughly one-fifth range since 1993. Canada's largest city, Toronto, has had about one-third women on its metropolitan council for more than ten years. The last time an elected woman premier held office was 1996, when Catherine Callbeck stepped down as leader of the Prince Edward Island Liberals.

Even worse, we find indicators of outright decline. Brian Mulroney appointed six women to his cabinet in 1984. Stephen Harper's cabinet in summer 2008 included only five female ministers. Men have led all the major parties at the federal level since 2003, when Alexa McDonough resigned from the top post in the New Democratic Party (NDP). In terms of the substance of public debate, when was the last time you heard a senior civic leader of any partisan stripe, at any level of government, speak out passionately on the issue of violence against women? Poverty levels among households headed by single moms? Breast cancer? After all, it's not as if these problems have disappeared. And when was the last time you heard a public decision maker refer in an authoritative, credible way to political mobilization by any women's group, for any cause?

If yours is a more placid personality than mine, you might urge me at this juncture to have more patience. After all, significant social changes don't happen overnight. According to this line of thought, it takes time to ensure that 52 percent of the Canadian population exercises what political theorists call the full panoply of democratic citizenship rights. This includes the opportunity to vote in elections at all levels, contest public office, and hold the highest positions in the land. Yet a quick glance at history reminds us that an organized suffragist movement began shortly after Confederation, with the founding in 1877 of the Toronto Women's Literary Society. Not long afterwards, in 1892, two women won seats on the Toronto School Board. In 1916, Manitoba became the first province to extend the right to vote to women, which was followed by enfranchisement at the federal level for most women citizens during World War I.[1]

Beginning in the 1970s, specific groups dedicated to the cause of electing more women to public office arrived on the scene in Canada. They included Women for Political Action, the Feminist Party of Canada, Winning Women, the 51% Solution, the Committee for '94 and, most recently, Equal Voice. Each urged party leaders to recruit more female candidates to run in provincial and federal elections. In some cases, the groups organized their own training sessions and conferences designed to ensure that well-qualified women were ready to take up the challenges of public life.

If it takes time to get more comfortable with women and political power together, then how much time is needed beyond the more than 130 years since 1877, or the roughly 35 years since the founding of Women for Political Action in 1972?

Perhaps you subscribe to the "pipeline theory," which is a scholarly twist on the patience argument. It says we need to wait until more women who have earned degrees in the fields that feed into public life reach senior enough career stages to be noticed by party recruiters. This sounds plausible, except that data from Statistics Canada show that the proportions of females holding positions as lawyers, business managers, and physicians have risen dramatically since the 1970s, reaching roughly 50 percent in many of these areas.[2] If large numbers of them were going to work their way up the political ladder, then we'd have seen signs of their imminent arrival by now.

Let's try a third tack. Maybe the prescription for progress goes back to family circumstances. Home responsibilities obviously limit what new parents can do beyond caring for small children and holding down paid work, and thus few can get involved in community activities or building political party networks. Maybe we need to wait for more women with grown children to emerge in the general population, so more of them have time to enter politics.

But demographic research suggests we should have already seen a rush at the floodgates. If the aging of the baby boomers and the maturation of the boomer echo generation offered a miraculous cure to reverse women's disengagement, then we'd see changes by now. Apparently, declining responsibilities for young children have not produced a bumper crop of political aspirants.

One problem with the waiting-for-older-children argument is revealed in time study research, which confirms what casual observation of the letters-to-the-editor page reveals when we open a daily newspaper. Research shows Canadian women continue to enjoy significantly less leisure time across their lifespan than do men—primarily because women spend more of their waking hours on unpaid work.[3] On average, females shoulder more complex tasks that involve other people, including more caring responsibilities for extended family members. From this perspective, there's no reason to believe that waiting for the boomers to mellow further will bring lots of women into politics.

I confess to having awaited the high tide of new recruits for at least 30 years. My fascination with politics and power began very early when, as a young child, I saw the charismatic smiles of the Kennedy brothers light up annual parades in my hometown of North Adams, Massachusetts. It was a promising moment on the cusp of Camelot, when Jack, Bobby, and Ted Kennedy projected the magnetism and charm that inspired hope in so many different people.

Why were their sisters so far from the limelight, though, and why were their wives so silent or, in Jacqueline's case, so breathless when they did speak? Growing up, I wondered what forces of spark, spunk, or luck propelled the few women without family connections who managed to make their way in politics. My fascination largely centred on Golda Meir, Shirley Chisholm, Geraldine Ferraro, Bella Abzug, and a remarkable Canadian named Rosemary Brown.

I later pursued these questions in a systematic way in the political science doctoral program at York University. In 1978, York was among the few universities in the world that encouraged graduate students to probe why so few women, ethno-cultural minorities, and young people were present in the top ranks of mainstream politics. Since the early 1980s, thanks to the support of a remarkable research culture at the University of Toronto, I've had the good fortune to study and teach about the political attitudes of women and men, their disparate patterns of party participation, and the impact of feminist movements on public policy in Canada, the United States, and Great Britain. This book draws on the first-hand experiences of female politicians and perspectives from gender and politics scholarship to ask why the numbers and voices of women in Canadian public life have in recent years become more muted instead of stronger.

The chapters that follow demonstrate the extent to which women continue to face daunting obstacles in their efforts to engage politically. I argue that the *women plus power equals discomfort* equation is revealed and reinforced regularly, notably in assessments of the leadership styles, personal appearances, and private lives of female politicians—which declare each to be somehow deficient. Moreover, the seeming success of past decades has ironically come to form yet another barrier: first, because we assume that lots of progress has already occurred, and second, because many women who reached top posts did so in circumstances that meant they could not succeed in the key way politicians win—namely, at the ballot box.

Consider, for example, the first woman premier in Canada. Rita Johnston became leader of the British Columbia Social Credit party in 1991, after her predecessor

(Bill Vander Zalm) resigned in disgrace following a scandal over the sale of his family-owned fantasy theme park. Hers was a poisoned chalice, a party leadership position irrevocably tainted by the Vander Zalm mess. We know in retrospect that the Social Credit party was on the brink of political extinction at the time, since it vanished soon afterwards as a player on the provincial scene.

Except for the absence of a fantasy theme park, the parallels between Johnston's experiences and those of Kim Campbell in the federal Progressive Conservative (PC) party are quite striking. Selected as PC leader after months and months of speculation about when the incumbent prime minister, Brian Mulroney, would resign because the popularity of both the party and his own leadership was on a steep slide downwards, Campbell took over a regime that had only weeks left in its mandate before an election had to be called. The split in the PC electoral coalition that saw the Reform party emerge in Western Canada and the Bloc Québécois form in Quebec meant the governing party faced bleak political prospects. Campbell briefly lifted Conservative spirits and polling numbers, but took the blame for what turned out to be a disastrous party showing in the 1993 federal elections.[4]

The fact that Johnston, Campbell, and others led their parties in hard times created a psychological association between women leaders and electoral loss. In Canada, the lesson that seemed to be drawn was as follows: parties should not choose women leaders because parties led by women both lose at the polls, and lose in extremis— sometimes to the point of disappearing altogether off the political radar screen. Women-led parties, in short, get shellacked by the opposition. To wit, the federal PCs spent about $20 million on their 1993 election campaign, won roughly 16 percent of the popular vote across the country, and elected precisely two MPs.[5] Campbell was not one of them; she lost in Vancouver Centre to the Liberal candidate, Hedy Fry.

As evidence presented in the next three chapters demonstrates, our peculiarly Canadian tendency to associate women politicians with loss and failure exists alongside a general discomfort with the juxtaposition of women and power, which we share with many other political systems. Chapter 2 explores our collective unease, and particularly the unease of political journalists, with the leadership styles of women in public life. Female politicians can't seem to get things right: whether they are assertive and confident, or consensual and team-oriented, they are found to be lacking in whatever it is that constitutes "the right stuff" of public authority.

Chapter 3 examines treatments of the physical attributes of female politicians, including efforts by journalists of both sexes to evaluate minute details of their dress and speech patterns. These assessments are typically grounded in plus-perfect expectations of what women in politics should wear or how their voices should sound, which are inevitably dashed in the face of perceived flaws, mistakes, and other imperfections. Chapter 4 unpacks our long-standing obsession with the sex lives of women in public life. This particular dimension of the *discomfort equation* picks apart individuals who deviate from the standard model of a married, heterosexual woman, and declares each to be either too chaste, too rowdy, or otherwise too distant from the presumed ideal type.

Taken together, public dissections of the leadership styles, personal styles, and sex lives of female politicians trivialize their contributions, and convert political women into little more than devalued cannon fodder for a relentless makeover project. Moreover, by concluding that no individual has the correct leadership style, or the right wardrobe and voice, or the proper romantic life, these portrayals contribute to a sense that there's not much talent out there, and that women as a group are simply not up to the task of top public service. In this way, the combination of plus-perfect expectations, followed by damning indictments that declare every individual has fallen short, work to reinforce an underlying disconnect between women and political power.

My shorthand expression for the psychological environment thus created is captured in a simple phrase: *women plus power equals discomfort*. This equation refers to a specific normative climate that says either no woman is good enough to be a public leader, or else no normal woman is (or would ever want to be) powerful. In Canada, the close association between female politicians at the apex of weak parties, and the electoral defeats suffered by those parties, has confounded the logical rebuttal to this equation. It's hard to argue that lots of women are good enough to hold top positions, because so many of them have led unsuccessful parties under disastrous circumstances. Moreover, efforts to recruit more female candidates often fall short once the individuals being wooed start to think about what happened to the few courageous pioneers who preceded them.

By themselves, these challenges are serious enough. Yet they are compounded in Canada by pervasive messages from both the political right and the left that say mainstream politics is irrelevant; this notion in turn depresses citizens' participation in elections, parties, and so on. The rise of the social right has particularly distanced women from power—by asserting they belong in the private home rather than the public sphere. In addition, Chapter 5 lays out the decline of an effective, parliamentary-focused feminist movement on the other side of the political spectrum, which would take on these interests and insist that women plus mainstream power together form an essential part of the democratic calculus.

This study concludes that we need to dismiss comfortable assumptions that say things are moving along swimmingly. Clinging to older views that urge more patience, more education, and so on, means we neither acknowledge nor interrogate present circumstances, and become stuck in a hopeful fog that may be reassuring but remains dangerously misguided. Chapter 6 offers an entirely different approach: eight concrete, doable reforms of both the formal and informal variety. These proposals are grounded in a view that like any other well-entrenched pattern, the *women plus power equals discomfort* nexus can be identified and changed, much as we strive to alter our eating habits and exercise routines from not-so-healthy to better ones.

You might well ask, "What's wrong with believing the status quo is okay? What are the real-world consequences of our unease with women and power together?" For starters, this phenomenon narrows the flow of promising politicians in one of the world's most stable, socially egalitarian, and widely-admired democracies. It creates obstacles that limit the ability of talented individuals to make their way through the political thicket—not to mention their willingness to even enter the thicket in the first place. After all, intelligent people are rarely so foolish as to throw themselves into circumstances that are stacked against them. We know from scholarly research that the supply of women who actively seek public roles remains small, and is unlikely to grow without significant changes of the sort proposed in Chapter 6.[6]

If we shift gears to the demand side of the story, assuming everything is fine muffles important arguments about women's importance to democratic life. For some time, we have permitted to reign uncontested claims that the quality and quantity of public engagement are at best unimportant, which in turn has let political parties off the hook in recruiting more women to top jobs. In addition, leaving the *women plus power equals discomfort* equation in place offers commentators a licence to continue to dissect and find fault with those few brave individuals who do step forward. In this way, our own political inertia cuts off promising avenues of reform that would alter the ways in which female politicians are recruited to public life, and then are portrayed and evaluated once they become more involved.

What's so valuable about public engagement? Why does women's participation matter to contemporary democracy? Scholars in this field often build on the work of political theorist Hanna Pitkin. Writing in the late 1960s, Pitkin maintained that the fabric of civic life depends on both the calibre of elected leaders and the strength of their ties with the public at large.[7] Her work highlighted the distinction between what she termed descriptive or "standing for" representation—meaning a demographic similarity between elected and electors—and substantive or "acting for" representation, which required a policy-based linkage between citizens and political leaders.

From the perspective of descriptive representation, women's presence as public actors confirms, while their absence weakens, the legitimacy of basic democratic practices. Women make up more than half of the population of Canada and of most other advanced industrial systems. As well, they generally comprise at least one-half of other politically under-represented groups, including ethno-cultural minorities, aboriginal peoples, and sexual orientation minorities. At the basic level of fairness, institutions in which percentages of female participants resemble those in the general public strike us as more politically credible than others where proportions of women fall far short of their numbers in the overall population.

For each of us as citizens, descriptive representation also resonates at the level of political symbolism. Seeing significant percentages of women in public life suggests to every observer, including small children, that both genders can contribute to that realm. Women politicians, for example, might inspire young girls to consider legislative careers. Their presence can shape cultural perceptions in such a way as to undermine stereotypes that say only men belong in public roles, while women are properly restricted to private ones. Political organizations are able to benefit from symbolic efforts to enhance female participation, since simply talking about recruiting more women can widen the party base and open the doors to new, more diverse sources of talent.

Seeing ethno-cultural minority representatives in elective office in the same proportion as their presence in the general population would provide parallel cues about opportunities for diverse groups of Canadians. As we can extrapolate from research by Sujit Choudhry and Michael Pal, visible minority women face considerable obstacles given their concentration in Canada's fastest-growing urban areas, which in turn are highly under-represented in provincial and federal legislatures.[8] Aboriginal women are also few and far between in Canadian politics, even though many hold significant leadership positions in their home communities.

At least two other reasons help explain why women's political presence matters. One follows from research on the tenor of debate in political groups and institutions, which shows that higher proportions of women are associated with lower levels of political conflict, greater emphasis on collective consensus-building, and higher standards of interpersonal respect. Scholars who compare different political environments observe the more reasonable and more collegial, less adversarial and less conflictual tenor of debate in spaces where women hold a significant proportion of seats. Although no precise figure defines a meaningful presence or "critical mass" of women in politics, representation over about 35 percent tends to alter the climate, conduct, and content of group debate.[9]

A second reason is grounded in political justice claims for equity in participation. These arguments maintain that women in politics matter because their presence (or lack thereof) serves as a barometer of basic fairness. As far back as Aristotle and others in the classical political theory tradition, citizen voice and representation have underpinned core Western definitions of what constitutes democracy. From this vantage point, women's absence highlights their lack of influence in public forums, and reminds us of barriers to access that face participants from different backgrounds. Representative democracy seems impaired, partial, and unjust when women, as a majority of citizens, fail to see themselves reflected in the leadership of their polity, and when men, as a minority of citizens, control most levers of power. Justice arguments, in short, focus attention on women's right to participate in public decision making, and their ability to do so without having to surmount discriminatory barriers.

Finally, Pitkin's discussion foreshadowed a significant body of scholarly work on the issue priorities of female politicians. Conducted primarily during the 1980s and following in North America and Western Europe, this research found that elected women were on average more liberal and more committed to the policy claims of

second-wave feminism than were their male counterparts. Studies of the substantive interventions of women
legislators, for example, tended to support Pitkin's view
of an important "acting for" dimension in political
representation.[10]

These empirical findings meant efforts to elect more
women in Canada were often defended as a way to enhance
the clout of organized feminism. Early research in the field
helped to underpin this strategy; as more women legislators
were elected between the 1970s and early 1990s, and more
women cabinet ministers were appointed, more pro-
feminist policies were enacted at both federal and provincial
levels. Among the highest percentages ever of women in a
government caucus or cabinet were those in the Ontario
NDP between 1990 and 1995, led by Premier Bob Rae.
His caucus included 20 women (out of 74 members, or
27 percent), at least half of whom had been active in
second-wave feminist organizations.[11] Rae appointed
11 women to his cabinet of 26 members, meaning women
held 42.3 percent of the portfolios.

What did the Ontario NDP government accomplish? It
widened child-care provision, increased funding for
shelters for battered women, raised the minimum wage,
strengthened pay equity laws, and legalized midwifery.
Even though leading women's groups wanted more policy
action of this type, the numbers-to-policy record of the
Rae years remains clear. No Ontario government before or
since had as many women in caucus and cabinet positions,
and no other government was as responsive to feminist
groups on the policy side.[12]

Before 1993, at the federal level, most women elected to
the House of Commons were NDP, Liberal, or Progressive
Conservative, and most of them were sympathetic toward
the issue positions of second-wave feminism. As in other

political systems, women's movement beliefs were closely associated with left–right attitudes and with party identification; among female legislators, NDP members tended to be more pro-feminist than Liberals, and Liberals more than PCs. That being said, studies consistently demonstrated that before 1993, NDP, Liberal, and PC women MPs worked together on such issues as promoting the constitutional rights of women, preventing violence against women, and strengthening gun-control legislation.[13]

The ability to build all-party consensus, however, declined in 1993 and following with the arrival in the House of Commons of right-wing Reform MPs mostly from Western Canada, who rejected the view that women were a politically relevant interest. The Reform party and its successor organizations, notably the Canadian Alliance and merged Conservative organizations, consistently maintained that territory was the country's single overarching, politically salient cleavage. The decentralist views of Canada's new political right carried with them other profoundly conservative positions that were at odds with those of organized feminism. After 1993, MPs from right-wing parties actively promoted—whether explicitly or implicitly—an anti–government intervention, anti-debt, anti-deficit, anti–Charter of Rights and Freedoms, anti–reproductive choice, and anti–homosexual rights agenda that merged economic laissez-faire ideas with the "family values" norms of social conservatism.

Given the contrast between these ideas and second-wave feminist beliefs, it's not surprising that relatively few women ran as Reform, Alliance, or merged Conservative party candidates, or won seats as MPs for those parties.[14] Moreover, right-wing formations grew comparatively weak roots among women voters, even in their home regions.[15] As I show in Chapter 5, the presence of this political stream in Parliament since 1993, and particularly the election of a Conservative minority government in 2006 and again in 2008, made it hard to advance pro-feminist policies at the federal level. Socially conservative men and women, holding the traditional view that the appropriate female role is in the home and not in politics, became increasingly influential during the years since 1993, and offered a new layer of meaning for the *women plus power equals discomfort* equation.

Returning to Pitkin's thesis, the presence of socially conservative women in Canadian legislatures provides an obvious reason to revisit the substantive representation ("acting for") argument. Since not all elected women are pro-equality advocates, we need to question the unrealistic expectation that numbers alone will produce progressive policy changes. It's crucial to consider closely the party origins and issue positions of candidates who seek our support, regardless of their gender. Canadians who want to advance even the most bare-bones version of egalitarian democracy, let alone more transformative versions of it, would do well to pressure party leaders so that their views are better known and directly pursued by those leaders. I return to this dimension of the representation challenge in Chapter 6.

Women, Power, Politics begins with the view that civic participation is the cornerstone of representative democracy, and asks how current circumstances have diverged so dramat-ically from what we expect. It reveals a fascinating story about our unease with public power that has, to this point, been told only partially—mostly through bits and pieces of political memoirs and in the arcane details of academic research. My goal is to make that material come alive, using perspectives about Canadian politicians to show why we should care about the fabric of contemporary democracy, and how we can build a more egalitarian future for our country.

Notes

1. Quebec women won the right to vote in provincial elections in 1940, while aboriginal women were granted the vote at the federal level only in 1960. See http://www.elections.ca/eca/eim/article_search/article.asp?id=26&lang=e&frmPageSize=&textonly=false, consulted 22 October 2007.

2. See *Women in Canada 2000: A Gender-Based Statistical Report* (Ottawa: Statistics Canada, 2000), 107.

3. See http://www.nwtsrc.com/content/news/statistics/09_who_participates_in_active_leisure.pdf, consulted 22 October 2007.

4. On poll numbers for Mulroney and Campbell, see David McLaughlin, *Poisoned Chalice: The Last Campaign of the Progressive Conservative Party?* (Toronto: Dundurn, 1994), 63–64, 92.

5. The Conservative national campaign cost about $10.4 million, and the general rule of thumb is that polling expenses plus local candidate spending not included in that figure would be at least as much. See David McLaughlin, *Poisoned Chalice*, 278.

6. See Louise Carbert, *Rural Women's Leadership in Atlantic Canada: First Hand Perspectives on Local Public Life and Participation in Electoral Politics* (Toronto: University of Toronto Press, 2006); Elizabeth Goodyear-Grant, "Crafting a Public Image: Women MPs and the Dynamics of Media Coverage," in Sylvia Bashevkin, ed., *Opening Doors Wider: Women's Political Engagement in Canada* (Vancouver: UBC Press, 2009), 17–66.

7. See Hanna Fenichel Pitkin, *The Concept of Representation* (Berkeley: University of California Press, 1967), 11.

8. See Sujit Choudhry and Michael Pal, "Is Every Ballot Equal? Visible Minority Vote Dilution," *IRPP Choices* 13:1 (2007), 1–30.

9. See Marian Sawer, Manon Tremblay, and Linda Trimble, "Introduction: Patterns and Practice in the Parliamentary Representation of Women," in Sawer, Tremblay, and Trimble,

eds., *Representing Women in Parliament: A Comparative Study* (London: Routledge, 2006), 18–20.

10. See Sawer et al., eds., *Representing Women in Parliament*, part 2; Debra L. Dodson, *The Impact of Women in Congress* (Oxford: Oxford University Press, 2006); Beth Reingold, *Representing Women: Sex, Gender, and Legislative Behavior in Arizona and California* (Chapel Hill: University of North Carolina Press, 2000); and Michele L. Swers, *The Difference Women Make: The Policy Impact of Women in Congress* (Chicago: University of Chicago Press, 2002).

11. See Sandra Burt and Elizabeth Lorenzin, "Taking the Women's Movement to Queen's Park: Women's Interests and the New Democratic Government of Ontario," in Jane Arscott and Linda Trimble, eds., *In the Presence of Women: Representation in Canadian Governments* (Toronto: Harcourt, Brace, 1997), 209.

12. See Lesley Byrne, "Making a Difference When the Doors are Open: Women in the Ontario NDP Cabinet, 1990–1995," in Bashevkin, ed., *Opening Doors Wider*, 93–107.

13. See Lisa Young, *Feminists and Party Politics* (Vancouver: UBC Press, 2000).

14. See Lisa Young, "Fulfilling the Mandate of Difference: Women in the Canadian House of Commons," in Arscott and Trimble, eds., *In the Presence of Women*, 84; Jacquetta Newman and Linda A. White, *Women, Politics, and Public Policy: The Political Struggles of Canadian Women* (Toronto: Oxford University Press, 2006), 116–117.

15. On the background to this gender gap, see Sylvia B. Bashevkin, *Toeing the Lines: Women and Party Politics in English Canada*, 2nd ed. (Toronto: Oxford University Press, 1993), chap. 2.

2

Discomfort Zones

So many years after Canadian women were granted the rights to vote and to hold public office, how could anyone suggest that Canadians remain uncomfortable with women and power together?

In fact, the broad contours of our social environment seem to offer near-perfect conditions for women to rise to the top as public leaders. Every year, lots of young women graduate not just from post-secondary educational institutions, but also from law, business, medicine, and other professional faculties. Canada boasts a relatively low birth rate, meaning the presence of young children at home poses a fairly weak barrier to the political participation of most adults.

At the federal level since 2003 and in many provinces as well, campaign finance reforms have made access to money less of an obstacle to running for office. Organizations devoted to encouraging more women to stand for public office, and to pressuring parties to nominate female candidates, have been part of our political scene since the early 1970s. Attitudinal research shows Canadians hold among the world's most egalitarian social values. Men here say they are more willing and more likely, for example, to assist with housework and child care than their counterparts in many other countries. According to multiple surveys, our willingness to defer to male authority figures has declined markedly over time.[1]

The terms under which our political system was created also seem conducive to women's engagement. Canada's origins as a federal political system—which was designed to accommodate different religious, linguistic, and regional interests—ensured that compromise and moderation became well-established hallmarks of public decision making. The consensus-oriented traditions of First Nations peoples helped to reinforce this emphasis, and to ensure that the recognition of group rights became a central tenet of our political culture.

Openness to newcomers also features to some degree in Canadian history, perhaps because of the difficulties of settling and inhabiting a harsh frontier landscape. Although questions continue to be raised about what it means in practice, multiculturalism as a theory underpins common views in Canada: immigration is central to the country's development, and strong public- and private-sector organizations are built on diverse teams of individuals—in which the varied perspectives and experiences of participants combine to create nimble, flexible, and responsive decision making. In addition, Canada has a long history of firm civil society control over a relatively weak military, as well as a fairly well-entrenched preference for social accommodation over conflict when it comes to resolving internal disputes.

Why do these factors seem so conducive to women's political mobility? First, by positing that supple, porous cultural norms are preferable to rigid, closed ones, Canadian values appear very open toward women and other traditionally under-represented groups entering politics. Second, these norms contain an implicit expectation that parties will proactively seek new political recruits from diverse backgrounds. Third, women may be especially advantaged as political participants by a long-standing normative emphasis in Canada on responsive, team-oriented skills, which are generally seen to be stronger in females than in males.[2] Fourth, as a middle-power country with a parliamentary system (in contrast to the superpower republic to our south), Canada is a place where public leaders have not usually been selected on the basis of their ability to wage wars or lead large international coalitions; also, unlike US presidents and governors, our prime ministers and premiers are not elected directly by nationwide or provincewide vote.[3]

With so many signposts pointing in positive directions, it's hard to explain the plateaus and even backward motion described in Chapter 1. Clearly, there must be something else going on, alongside the patterns we've reviewed thus far.

This chapter unpacks the first box of evidence labelled *women plus power equals discomfort*. In particular, it shows how journalists, political insiders, and we as citizens are often uneasy with seeing women as public leaders, with females and authority together in the same picture frame. The material presented here reveals an unsettling habit whereby we pick apart the leadership styles of female politicians, only to conclude they are seriously lacking in one respect or another. This relentless dissection process, I argue, makes it well-nigh impossible for women leaders to operate effectively, dissuades talented individuals from pursuing political careers, and reduces the likelihood that average citizens will feel comfortable with seeing women on top.

As a corollary to this proposition, I suggest that when we do group women and power together in Canada, we unfortunately gravitate toward an image of female political leaders as incurable losers. This pattern is not surprising given that when Canadian women rose to the top, they generally did so in weak or uncompetitive political parties—including some that were frankly lost-cause, or, to be very Canadian, "wilderness" organizations in terms of their distance from government power. By definition, any person who leads a lost-cause party is expected to lose elections. Yet female politicians in Canada have been collectively branded as failures because of their close association with the leadership of weak parties.

Let me reiterate that what I'm proposing is explicitly *not* a conspiracy theory about men. In fact, it's clear that both women and men remain not only queasy about having women atop the political heap, but also willing to adopt doomsday scenarios that paint female political leaders as the civilian equivalents of crash-and-burn kamikaze pilots.

Are Public Values the Problem?

The answer to this question, stated simply, is no. Canadians have consistently expressed among the world's most open-minded views about their willingness to vote for parties led by women and for local candidates who are female.

My thesis therefore hinges on the important but often neglected gap between what large-scale public surveys and census studies say about our beliefs and opportunities in aggregate, and how we operate as individuals in our day-to-day interactions. Surveys can tell us a great deal about the broad contours of public values, but they are of limited use in explaining specific actions and experiences in the real world. They may shed light on helpful groundwork or a precondition for social change (in this case women's upward mobility in politics) but by no means do the attitudes they tap offer sufficient foundations for that change to take effect.

Pollsters have reported, for example, that about 50 percent of Canadians on a given day said the country would be better off if more women held public office.[4] This can be interpreted as meaning that half of the adult population wants to elect more female politicians, and would be prepared to vote for them as candidates. Such a result is extremely promising at the level of political potential, since it suggests a degree of openness and, indeed, positive bias toward women that is a necessary precondition for civic equality.

What this finding does not reveal, however, is at least as important. Survey data on general questions cannot reflect how we as citizens, or how media commentators and party hierarchs, will respond to particular individuals who seek to make their way in public life. What if, despite all the egalitarian values in the world, we end up tagging women leaders as hopeless losers? Or what if (as I argue in Chapter 3) the voices of female legislators are analyzed and reanalyzed by political commentators, and deemed shrill, poorly modulated, or otherwise ineffectual? What if the prospect of being daily put under a microscope itself deters women who might otherwise consider entering politics?

Survey questions also may tell us little about the importance or salience of an issue. Let's return to the 50 percent of poll respondents who said the country would be better off with more women in politics. These responses, however honest and sincere they may be, don't reveal the significance of political equality for those who answered the question in an egalitarian way. We don't know how far individual respondents would go toward ensuring women in the parties they support have a fair chance at moving up. After all, very few interviewees in a random national sample are likely to hold party membership, follow politics closely between elections, or know very much about how people climb the greasy pole inside parties.

Obviously, a lack of political involvement limits the ability of even the most fair-minded survey respondent to take direct action to help a woman to advance in public life. Moreover, the half of respondents in the survey who expressed divergent views on the benefit of women in politics could be far more vocal, organized, and committed to opposing women's political engagement than the half who expressed support for women politicians. While members of the latter group might feel quite secure in their belief that Canada is a fair and open society in which any talented person can succeed, those in the former category might be more motivated and mobilized to keep women in their traditional roles—that is, far from positions of political responsibility.

This inability to discern real-world consequences from poll results parallels the disjuncture between levels of formal education and opportunities in public life. Raw attitudinal data, in this analogy, offer the equivalent of a very preliminary starting point; they are the words people say when the cost of making a statement is extremely low. "Talk is cheap," so to speak, when we don't have to back up what we say with any form of meaningful action.

Similarly, Statistics Canada data show about 55 percent of Canadian women work for pay, and that roughly half of recent law and business school graduates are female.[5] These figures about post-graduate diplomas clearly do not mean the pathway to professional achievement is smoothly paved for each individual who filled out a questionnaire about education and occupation. In particular, the ability to convert work experience, especially in law or business, into assets for a political career may continue to vary considerably between women and men, no matter how many females are employed in the so-called "pipeline" professions.

The distance between rhetoric and raw data on one side, and reality on the other, is often brought home when politicians promise one thing during an election campaign, and do something else entirely after they win office. Elsewhere we find a similar gap. Leaders of large organizations can commit themselves on paper to some significant vision or goal, and then offer little or no support for the individuals who work with them to reach the stated objective. For example, senior executives in a large corporation might say they want more diverse people in top ranks, and appoint a few women to positions of significant responsibility, but end up treating those women in ways that are inconsistent with their own rhetoric. Revealing indicators of the gap between talk and action in this last case could involve removing positions held by women from the organization's major networking loop, or assessing the contributions of female executives in ways that say more about the discomfort of the male evaluators than the performance of the females who report to them. The fact that the number of women in top corporate positions in Canada has dropped in recent years attests to ongoing difficulties in women's leadership beyond the sphere of public office.[6]

Qualms about Leadership

At its heart, the *women plus power equals discomfort* phenomenon is grounded in a zone of social unease that's characterized by sometimes intangible, but nevertheless significant, markers. These markers often relate to the idea of leadership itself, which remains in many respects a masculine concept that constrains women's ability to "fit the bill" in elite-level politics. To cut straight to the chase, as American politics scholar Meredith Conroy points out, "The traditional view of women rejects the idea that femaleness and political power can coexist."[7] Moreover, we don't need to be full-blown traditionalists to retain vestiges of this perspective.

My dictionary defines *leadership* both as the position of leader, which in turn is defined as "a guiding or directing head," and as the ability to lead, meaning "to command or direct (an army or other large organization)."[8] The questions raised by these definitions include: How comfortable are we with seeing women in authoritative roles, where they lead other people? Are we prepared to be one of the cabinet ministers, civil servants, or citizens who is directed by a female political executive?

"Well," you might reply, "good leadership as we've come to understand it in Canada has more to do with guidance and team-building than with issuing orders. Consensual leadership, whether exercised by women or men, is okay."

Our unease with defining consensus-building as leadership, and with seeing women employ the coercive levers of public authority, rests at the crux of the *discomfort equation*. It recalls the work of New York–based psychologist Virginia Valian, who maintains we carry around "intuitive hypotheses about the behaviors, traits, and preferences of men and women, boys and girls," which she terms "gender schemas."[9] Valian argues that more than 100 years after first-wave feminists campaigned for the rights to vote, hold public office, and set up their own bank accounts, North American attitudes about what constitutes properly male and female behaviour remain quite traditional.

In the realm of political leadership, she posits, gender stereotypes continue to shape the public presentation of female office-holders. Even though we no longer wrap baby girls exclusively in pink and baby boys in blue, we routinely read and watch accounts of female politicians that portray them as ill-suited outsiders in public life, thus placing women far from the competitive mainstream. This distancing takes place in large part through the ways in which news information is chosen, interpreted, and then presented to us, which together make up what communications researchers term "media framing." In the words of Pippa Norris, a women and politics scholar based at Harvard University, news frames are "interpretive structures that set particular events within their broader context. In this sense, news frames give 'stories' a conventional 'peg' to arrange the narrative, to make sense of the facts, to focus the headline, and to define events as newsworthy. Frames provide contextual cues giving order and meaning to complex problems, actions, and events."[10]

An extensive body of international research demonstrates the significance of the ways in which politicians are presented to us. Summarizing the burgeoning American literature in this field, political scientist David Niven writes: "Media coverage of congressional candidates and incumbents has been found to influence recognition, emotional connections, evaluations, and, ultimately, vote choice." According to Niven, if commentaries about female participants focus on matters of style rather than substance, then they "serve as a distraction from the issue commitments elected officials seek to communicate. Of course, this attention can also be belittling as it suggests the superfluity of women elected officials' concerns or undermines their professional stature by dwelling on their physical stature."[11]

In Canadian politics, the framing process conveys a decisive impression that women lack appropriate leadership, personal appearance, speech styles, and romantic lives. It deflects attention away from the substantive content of women's ideas, policies, and contributions, and conveniently diverts us from noticing how far we have *not* come. Canadians, for instance, have yet to witness a federal budget speech delivered by a woman minister of finance. We have yet to see a federal leaders' debate during an election campaign with all-women panels of both politicians and journalists, even though we routinely see all-men panels of leaders and reporters.

As citizens, we've not been encouraged or inspired during recent years to interrogate the frames established by leading interpreters of mainstream politics. Few eyebrows are raised when celebrity-style dissections of individuals become the main cannon fodder for political discussions in the media. Thus these assessments take on an air of legitimacy and leave us as citizens to sift through and frequently mimic the same perspectives. Valian's thesis shows us how gender schemas centred around personalities serve to define and, in many respects, limit the parameters of both expert and everyday political conversation. Media framing that adopts this approach serves at least one purpose—to draw attention away from major lapses of democracy, equality, and representation—so what we end up hearing and often imitating is a great deal of gossip-laden talk and not much analytically incisive thinking about civic life.

How do gender schemas find their way into the media framing of women politicians? Simply stated, according to Valian, our intuitive hypotheses ensure that similarly talented males and females experience the same organizational circumstances differently. In her words, prevailing gender schemas mean "women do not reliably profit from their competence, strategic analysis, and effort to the same extent men do."[12] Moreover, using different schemas to evaluate male and female contributions is particularly crucial when individual talents are on public display. The realm of politics is thus different than that of private sector corporations or large educational institutions including university faculties, for example, where we can measure outcomes fairly precisely and reliably via profits on the balance sheet or books and articles on a curriculum vitae.

By way of contrast, public leadership is all about large-scale intangible qualities, such as inspiring confidence and trust, charting visions for a large and diverse society, and making hopes and dreams for a country's future become a reality. Since the absence of firm metrics such as profits or publications means every armchair observer can not only introduce but also calibrate a performance indicator, almost the only actual test we can all agree on is what happens at election time. Did Leader A offer a convincing vision of Canada's future? Could Leader B inspire confidence and trust? To what degree did voters connect with Leader C's roadmap from dream to reality?

If we apply Valian's concept of gender schemas to the evaluation of female politicians, then we see how even a slight sense of ambivalence about gender and authority will distort media framing. Leadership qualities can be ignored, obscured, or underestimated by people who remain uncomfortable with seeing women command and direct. For instance, evaluators might not want to see a woman take charge in a forceful way of Canada's economy or armed forces; at the same time they might undervalue her "soft-side" leadership skills of guidance and team building. As Norris reminds us, "gendered news frames may combine and thereby reinforce a range of sex stereotypes"; in some instances, they can turn out to be "an electoral liability, if women are framed as inexperienced outsiders, and if voters feel that they need practiced leaders to deal with serious problems."[13]

Leaders, as the dictionary definition states, are expected to lead. This very assumption places women in what Valian terms "an impossible position." In her words, "when women actively adopt an assertive leadership style, they are perceived more negatively than men...Evaluators see leadership and professional ability as masculine traits that are evaluated more positively when displayed by men than when displayed by women."[14] Females who have experienced first-hand the limits imposed by gender schemas often avoid aggressive command-and-control approaches, and instead develop nurturing, consensual, and team-oriented leadership styles. They, however, frequently confront other difficulties that follow from relying on "soft" leadership styles. According to Valian, "the more a woman is perceived as a woman the less likely it is that she will be perceived as professionally competent. The qualities required of leaders and those required for femininity are at odds with each other."[15] By behaving in ways that appear sensitive, expressive, and task-oriented, women are often not recognized as leaders.[16]

Valian's conclusion, based on her macro-level analysis of hundreds of psychology experiments, observational studies, and focus groups, is hardly reassuring. It is particularly troubling in the case of political leadership, where perceptions and assessments of individuals float around in full public view and are based on few agreed-upon metrics other than the ability to win elections. In fact, her thesis suggests that tensions between norms of leadership and gender schemas on one side and women's ability to hold top political positions on the other are so deeply rooted that they could potentially prevent us from ever reaching parity in the polity.

Probing Our Qualms about Leadership

Some of the most blatant bits of evidence that we can't quite come to grips with women as assertive, directive bearers of public authority emerge in everyday conversation. The term "ball-buster" sums up much of the pervasive trepidation that is related to women and power together: it's a sexually charged term evocative of male castration caused by female empowerment, which emerges in different contexts. Sometimes we hear the expression when people are pushed beyond their comfort zones in social situations, and perceive confident women as bossy, strident, pushy, or otherwise incompletely socialized to traditional feminine norms. At other times, this nomenclature rises to the surface in professional settings when women's leadership or speaking styles seem more direct or confident than conventional norms have deemed appropriate.

Our language that betrays unease, however, is not restricted to sexualized images. It's hard not to notice the frequent use of first-name references to female politicians, whether in media accounts or everyday conversation. While this practice makes political women seem approachable and folksy, it carries some clear disadvantages. First-name references trivialize individual women by suggesting they are familiar gals-from-around-the-corner, rather than public officials who have earned our respect for their faith, at least, in the democratic process. In Canada, we've heard for decades from senior political commentators about Flora, Kim, Sheila, and Belinda, plus we've absorbed constant spillover from south of the border about Bella, Hillary, and so on.

For more than 20 years, I have had the good fortune to teach talented students at the University of Toronto, and to work with many reporters from a variety of media organizations. But each time students or journalists telephone or email me to discuss a woman politician, the message almost always includes a first-name reference to the subject of their interest. When I respond, I insist on asking whether we're also going to discuss leading men in politics using the same nomenclature, since I'm not on a first-name basis with either the men or the women we're talking about. Students and reporters, males and females alike, seem stunned. "What do you mean?" they ask. Simply stated, I point out, either we trivialize and familiarize all politicians, or we treat the women with the same respect we accord the men. Ouch. I can feel their phones or keyboards wiggle as they shift uncomfortably in their seats.

The purpose of my comment is to get us to think about the implications of the language we use. As my American colleague Caroline Heldman points out in her analysis of the political career of Hillary Clinton, using a woman's first name in public references is "infantilizing" because it connotes an absence of "power and legitimacy." Speakers may not hold any conscious intent to demean women in this way, but their rhetoric "has the 'real world' consequence of de-legitimizing knowledge, experience, and ultimately, leadership."[17]

The *women plus power equals discomfort* phenomenon is also revealed in the flip side of our style obsessions—which is a tendency to pay far less attention to the serious ideas and policy proposals of female politicians. If we were to subtract all the stories in the press about whether Ms. X was too confident, Ms. Y too diffident; Ms. A too well-dressed, Ms. B too plain; Ms. M too chaste and Ms. N too rowdy, we'd hardly find much coverage at all of women in politics. David Niven's quantitative, long-term study of newspaper stories about US congressional and Senate candidates reached the following stark conclusions: "women are afforded less respect by the media. In various measures, women are subject to fewer positive and more negative portrayals than men...Women are twice as likely to have age or appearance mentioned than men. Women are much more likely to have their personality or personal traits discussed than are men."[18]

What did any of the women stand for in terms of issue priorities? Which core beliefs and commitments led them to seek public office? We'd be unlikely to learn very much about serious policy ideas from a random sample of the Canadian television stories and newspaper clippings I've collected during recent decades. As I noted in Chapter 1, this overwhelming interest in matters other than political substance effectively limits the supply of women who are willing to run as candidates, since who would voluntarily subject herself to such sustained, invasive, and often trivial personal evaluation before the public eye? Moreover, because individual women can't escape the prevailing evaluation criteria, those who are already active have few choices other than quitting politics in order to escape the mélange of often conflicting messages about how to present themselves.

Canadian researchers who've spoken with prospective female politicians find that relatively few of them want to see every dimension of themselves—including their approaches toward working with other people, in addition to their voices, clothes, and romantic lives—dissected in full public view.[19] These women are often quite frustrated with the alternatives before them. Many are astute enough to realize that aside from causing a fundamental loss of personal privacy, constant exposure to a public and media circus (as we've seen with Hollywood celebrities) detracts from their ability to enjoy happy, balanced, and personally fulfilling lives.

As citizens of a democratic country, we who care about the quality of public life would ideally like to believe that people enter politics because they have good ideas about making the world a better place. Prospective candidates for elective office may want to strengthen Canada's health-care system, create more environmentally sustainable cities, or better target our development assistance to poor countries. How many women want to enter public life knowing that their substantive visions will be largely ignored, while they (and often their families as well) will be confined to a style-obsessed fishbowl?

At its heart, the *discomfort equation* creates confusion over precisely what we want in the way of leadership styles. Should political women be caring, nurturing, and motherly? In other words, can women get ahead in politics if they come across as unthreatening, deferential, and ready to consult widely on every issue? This approach is guaranteed not to offend anyone, except people who've read the basic dictionary definition and wonder, "What kind of leader is that?" Can we realistically expect leaders with "soft" styles of guidance and team building to make the tough decisions?

On the other side of the ledger, perhaps female politicians should go for broke and be assertive, confident, take-charge types. But we know this can send insecurity sensors into spasms. Valian's research on gender schemas tells us that such behaviour can be more than a bit threatening. Imagine a televised debate among party leadership candidates that involves at least one woman who's decisive, firm, and direct. If she wins the race for her party's top post, are we as citizens going to warm to her during the next election campaign and select her as our premier or prime minister? How will journalists present her to the public in their accounts?

These problems hold measurable consequences in the real world. For one thing, considerable evidence exists that Canada faces a serious shortage of potential female candidates. Research by Louise Carbert of Dalhousie University shows political parties confront major recruitment challenges, especially outside our large metropolitan centres. In cities including Toronto, Montreal, and Vancouver, the Liberals and New Democrats in particular have since the 1970s recruited a steady stream of female candidates who went on to win seats in the House of Commons.[20] If the failings of already weak parties are attributed back to the women who lead them, and if female politicians face style dissections in full public view, then it is not surprising that parties face a particularly hard time finding women from small-town and rural Canada who will run for public office. Without the size and cosmopolitan mass afforded by urban areas, which offer more opportunities for anonymity, these women confront head-on the unease and discomfort that characterize the life of female politicians.

Carbert's research zeroed in on other stark differences between what goes on in cities versus less densely settled areas. In order to identify the origins of this disparity, she spent time talking with local leaders in Atlantic Canada—a region where the percentages of women holding public office at all levels have generally fallen below our not-very-high national averages. One of the most memorable comments she heard came from a party recruiter who said promising individuals refuse to get involved because "We seem to eat our own women alive in this country." Other interviewees contended that Kim Campbell had been "set up" as the "'fall guy' for the party on its way down," and that former Saint John mayor Elsie Wayne faced no end of wardrobe scrutiny once she went to Ottawa as an MP. Carbert concluded that lots of women in Atlantic Canada were simply not willing to offer themselves up for what they saw as humiliating public consumption, no matter how assiduously they were courted by political parties.

Leadership Style Problems

This supply shortfall exists alongside a strange demand curve, whereby media commentators, political insiders, and the public seem to relish any opportunity to sit in judgment of female politicians. Valian's argument about gender schemas maintains it is difficult, or well-nigh impossible, for political women to find a leadership style that works. But what is it that makes us quite so edgy?

We know from political psychology research that every prospective candidate for public office needs some degree of confidence in order to enter politics in the first place, whether as a candidate for school board trustee, city councillor, or legislative member.[21] Memoirs written by female politicians reveal that many began to believe in themselves while working with other people on shared causes. The causes varied widely and included permitting welfare recipients to attend university so they could improve their employment prospects (which was key to Rosemary Brown's decision to seek office in British Columbia) or reforming mental health and children's rights policies (as Audrey McLaughlin tried to do in Ontario and the Yukon).[22]

A crucial problem with projecting confidence, even if for a public-spirited reason rather than for personal career advancement, is that this behaviour conflicts with traditional gender schemas that prescribe female deference and passivity. Assertive women risk being viewed and then portrayed in a negative way because they challenge our ingrained assumptions; that is, females with palpable ambition are often perceived as hyper-masculine, not properly socialized, and so on. These unabashedly strong women, as a result, may set off major alarm bells on the discomfort meter.

We don't need to go as far afield as British press portrayals of "Iron Lady" Margaret Thatcher to see how strong women can be framed as deviant. Canadian reporters offer fine illustrative examples on their own. For instance, in his account of UK prime minister Gordon Brown's July 2007 visit to the US capital, senior *Globe and Mail* columnist John Ibbitson compared the "gravelly" Brown with each of his predecessors. Ibbitson ticked them off as the "silken Tony Blair, strident Margaret Thatcher, suave Harold Macmillan or eloquent Winston Churchill."[23] Now if Thatcher had been silken, suave, eloquent, or gravelly, would she have become either Tory party leader or British prime minister? What was "strident" about her except that she was an assertive woman in a position usually held by assertive men?

Among the most memorable women in the Canadian House of Commons during recent decades was Hamilton, Ontario MP Sheila Copps. As a member of the small Liberal caucus during the first Mulroney government (1984–1988), Copps distinguished herself as a feisty "Rat Pack" debater who shouted, heckled, and consistently peppered Conservative ministers with tough questions. During one particularly heated parliamentary session, Copps got under the skin of federal justice minister John Crosbie, who had been accused of awarding a government job to his own son. Crosbie replied to Copps's heckling as follows: "Just quieten down, baby. You bunch of poltroons can shout all you like. The Rat Pack can quieten down. The titmice can quieten down."[24]

This exchange, and others like it, inspired Copps to write a popular book titled *Nobody's Baby*. The volume offered practical advice for women who sought to enter politics and face down the nasty insults. At no point in that text or her second book, *Worth Fighting For*, did she suggest it might have been better to adopt a more conciliatory public style. Copps realized that political women with her type of approach were consistently framed as over the top and out of control, and she continued to employ this political style because she presumably found it most suitable and effective for what she wanted to accomplish.

As a result, Copps was routinely framed in the media as both shrill and aggressive. One January 1990 editorial cartoon in *The Globe and Mail* portrayed her as a battle-scarred armoured soldier carrying both a hand grenade and a purse. In this same drawing, a male organizer in Copps's Liberal leadership campaign headquarters opens her helmet to report, "...Your early polls look encouraging...but there's still some work to do on image softening."[25] Writing a few months later in *The Toronto Star*, Joan Bryden reported that Copps had adopted a "more aggressive" debating style, ostensibly to challenge the party leadership front-runner, Jean Chrétien. According to Bryden, Chrétien's supporters "signaled their disapproval of her tactic with boos. What was previously described as feistiness and spirit was suddenly criticized as chippiness and arrogance." Bryden went on to describe at length examples of Copps's "combativeness and flashes of temper," as if neither of the other main Liberal contenders, Jean Chrétien and Paul Martin, possessed a whiff of either anger or ego.[26]

At the other end of the political style spectrum, women who adopt a consensual approach also face problems. They are often portrayed as weak, indecisive, and worst of all, lacking in leadership skills. The risk they confront is that by being deferential and consultative, their career prospects will be written off as nonexistent because niceness is seen as uncharismatic, lacking in content, and inappropriate on the parliamentary scene.

Consider the case of Audrey McLaughlin, the first woman to head a major Canadian federal party. McLaughlin was elected as NDP leader in 1989, to succeed Ed Broadbent. Her leadership campaign speeches advocated "a more open party and a more inclusive, consultative way of operating...Canadians were ready for a new kind of politics."[27] McLaughlin endorsed a different approach to public office, which she described as follows: "The real problem is that we've got the wrong kind of leadership, a bullying leadership that doesn't listen to anyone beyond the core of traditional power holders who serve no one's interests but their own. I want to lead in a different way: by listening carefully and helping pull open the doors to power."[28]

As the NDP seat count in the House of Commons began to plummet from 43 when McLaughlin became leader, to nine when she resigned in 1995, the political consensus about party leadership grew increasingly anti-consensus. That is, her style of seeking input from a wide variety of sources was viewed as possibly suitable in social work (McLaughlin's area of professional training) but as inappropriate for parliamentary politics. The general verdict about Canada's first female federal party leader was not promising: nice woman, good intentions, but essentially passive and ineffectual.

Analyses of media coverage of the 1993 federal election debates have unearthed much of the groundwork behind this impression. Elisabeth Gidengil of McGill University and Joanna Everitt of the University of New Brunswick examined in detail both the debates themselves and television news accounts of the debates. Their study found "McLaughlin's debating style in 1993 was much more low-key than any of the other leaders," who were Kim Campbell, Jean Chrétien, Preston Manning, and Lucien

Bouchard.[29] Since she did not employ attention-grabbing behaviours including intensely conflictual or otherwise surprising interventions, McLaughlin was widely ignored by other debaters and by media commentators. For example, even though she participated in both the French- and English-language debates, McLaughlin received minimal news coverage afterwards.

By way of contrast, PC party leader Kim Campbell participated in those same debates, and adopted an entirely different debating style. According to Gidengil and Everitt, "while Campbell was clearly the more combative of the two women who participated in the 1993 English-language debate, she was not obviously more aggressive than the men in the debate. Admittedly, she used the most aggressive type of debating behaviour, gesturing with her fist clenched, as often (12 times) as Chrétien (11 times). However, she ranked behind the men when it came to the other aggressive behaviours," which included interrupting other speakers and pointing a finger at them.[30]

Rather than being ignored afterwards by reporters, as McLaughlin was, "Campbell received the most coverage of all the leaders," according to Everitt and Gidengil.[31] But, like McLaughlin, Campbell was primarily addressed in media accounts according to subjective assessment criteria, rather than with factual descriptions of her role in the debates. This interpretive framing differed from that accorded to men, in that "statements made by the female leaders were less likely than those made by the male leaders to be left to speak for themselves."[32] According to Gidengil and Everitt, Campbell's performance was scrutinized more than that of other incumbent prime ministers or party leaders whose organizations experienced a steep descent during the same period; they link this difference to Campbell's novelty as our first female prime minister.

What did media analysts conclude in 1993? Quebec reporters and post-debate English TV commentators claimed Campbell lost both the French- and the English-language debate. Some focused on what was described as her "armed and ready," aggressive "attack mode."[33] These portrayals were hardly surprising, since Campbell's own advisors had counselled her "to violate traditional gender-role expectations" even though they risked, in media accounts, "having those behaviours overemphasized."[34] With opponents arrayed on both the right and the left, and with a clear need to attract media coverage, Campbell's political handlers believed she had no choice: "she had to occupy the centre ground by appearing moderate in position while attacking her opponents relentlessly...A subdued performance would confirm to the media a losing campaign. She had to rise above her opponents not by stealth or statesmanship, but by sheer force and persuasion."[35]

The disparate experiences of Audrey McLaughlin and Kim Campbell in 1993 neatly distilled the leadership style conundrum facing women in Canadian politics. For McLaughlin, avoiding high-voltage interventions in a debate meant being consigned to the margins—so that she and her party were sidelined far beyond the main stage. For Campbell, high-energy engagement in that forum meant being tagged as overly aggressive. Although the latter style received lots of press attention, it raised worries that the Conservative leader was in a defensive mode because her party was about to fall off a cliff.[36] In short, as the lead study in this field demonstrates, news coverage differed starkly from real-world actions because reportage "focuses disproportionately on combative behaviour by female party leaders, but tends to ignore the women when they adopt a more low-key style."[37]

Women as Losers

We can't feign surprise that because McLaughlin's term as NDP leader and Campbell's as PC leader produced no electoral breakthroughs for their parties—and, in fact, were periods of decline in both parties' seat counts—the *women plus power equals discomfort* equation took on a dangerous new twist. During a fairly short period of time, between roughly 1989 and 1993, female politicians went from being celebrated as freshness incarnate, with virtual halos over their heads as potential saviours of their beleaguered parties, to being castigated as losers who dragged those same parties to new depths. This slide meant political women seemed like witches rather than angels, and were seen as responsible for bad news rather than for political salvation.

Arguably the most invidious part of this loser syndrome was that it ignored the weak condition of Canadian parties led by women. Many female politicians who managed to reach the top of the parliamentary pyramid did so in parties that were uncompetitive to begin with. Most were chosen either to lead wilderness parties that had long been far from power, or to reverse the declining fortunes of once-competitive parties. Typically, the latter had reached a critical condition—and had entered what appeared to be an irreversible slide—some time before women leaders ever got the keys to the corner office.

Even if we look beyond the rarefied realm of party leadership, it becomes clear that female office-holders in general are often subjected to differential evaluative standards. For example, research on legislative candidacies in the US reveals stereotypical assumptions held by reporters that men are by definition more politically experienced, competent, and issue-focused in areas including the economy than are their female counterparts. In the words of David Niven, the upshot of this sustained pattern is that "women are afforded less respect by the media. In various measures, women are subject to fewer positive and more negative portrayals than men."[38] According to Canadian studies as well, the viability of female politicians has been questioned repeatedly, whether directly or indirectly, in prevailing news frames—meaning quite simply that "they are less likely than male contenders to be portrayed as winners."[39]

Our willingness in Canada to associate women with political defeat added another layer to the problem of gender schemas. The link between female politicians and electoral setbacks can serve as yet another reason for shielding, marginalizing, or excluding them from positions of public responsibility. The woman-as-loser view means female politicians can be portrayed as reliably unreliable, because they "screw up" and lead their parties toward a deep downward dive. In the words of Alberta-based polit-ical scientists Linda Trimble and Jane Arscott, "The revolving door for female leaders in Canada has recently expelled a number of experienced women from political life, reinforcing the view that women cannot succeed in the top jobs."[40]

This perspective may have already created a major demand problem in our system. Do party members avoid selecting candidates whose gender links them with a plunge toward the abyss, rather than a climb to new heights? On the supply side, will women voluntarily choose to enter politics, and make their ways upward through the ranks of a party, under the dark shadow of this loser imagery?

For more than a decade, the close tie between women leaders and weak electoral outcomes in Canada has cast an ominous glow. Where did it originate? At the federal level, all three women who have served as party leaders (New Democrats Audrey McLaughlin and Alexa McDonough, and Progressive Conservative Kim Campbell) led uncompetitive parties—in the sense that they were either far from power (in the case of the NDP) or unlikely to win re-election (in the case of the PCs). Campbell became leader when the public opinion standings of both her party and its incumbent leader, Brian Mulroney, were extremely weak. It's worth recalling that Mulroney's poll ratings were so low that they fell below the prime rate of interest, which was then considerably higher than it's been in subsequent years.[41] As Campbell poignantly recalled in her memoirs, party delegates in 1993 "were looking for a miracle worker to stop the Tories' slide into oblivion."[42]

The less-than-promising circumstances facing McLaughlin, McDonough, and Campbell meant none of them was likely to become prime minister. Yet the electoral debacles their parties experienced were particularly painful. The NDP seat count in the House of Commons dropped from 43 in 1989, when McLaughlin became leader, to 14 in 2003, when McDonough resigned. During Campbell's brief time as PC leader in 1993, the Conservatives reached their historic low of two MPs.

At the federal level, we unfortunately have no countervailing evidence to challenge the view that women leaders bring disastrous consequences. That's because in no case has a woman won the top post in a party that was electorally competitive, although many have tried. Female candidates contested the federal Liberal leadership in 1990 (Sheila Copps), 2003 (Copps again), and 2006 (Martha Hall Findlay); and ran for the Conservative top job in 1976 (Flora MacDonald) and 2004 (Belinda Stronach). None of these campaigns was successful. The men who won each race either became prime minister or, in the case of the

2006 Liberal leadership, had a reasonable chance of doing so in the future.

At the provincial level, women have led uncompetitive parties since the 1950s, when Thérèse Casgrain became head of the Quebec CCF. It's difficult to imagine a more formidable challenge than the one she faced: Casgrain was a committed feminist who led a socialist political party in the insular, conservative environment of Maurice Duplessis's Quebec. In fact, the Quebec CCF during the 1950s set a high-water mark for wilderness parties, since it failed to elect a single candidate to the National Assembly or to win even 1 percent of the popular vote in provincial elections.[43] Casgrain published a vivid book-length account of her experiences under the title *A Woman in a Man's World*. She was later appointed to the Senate of Canada, and is remembered for her principled commitment to both social reform and women's rights during an era when neither was terribly popular.

Since Casgrain's time, lots of other Canadian women have led marginal provincial parties. What's notable—but widely ignored—is the fact that many of them measurably improved their party's fortunes. In Western Canada, Joy Macphail served as interim leader of the BC NDP when it held precisely two seats in the provincial legislature. She was succeeded by Carole James—who boosted the party's seat count to 33.[44] As leader of the Alberta NDP during the 1990s, Pam Barrett raised that party's legislative representation from zero to two MLAs.[45] Lynda Haverstock worked hard to bring the Saskatchewan Liberals closer to political viability; during her time as leader from 1989 through 1995, the party grew from one seat to 11, and gained Official Opposition status.[46] As head of the Manitoba Liberals, Sharon Carstairs became the first woman in Canada to hold the position of leader of the Official

Opposition; her party broke through from one seat (her own) to 20 in the 1988 provincial elections.[47] In the Atlantic region, Alexa McDonough managed to increase the NDP's standing in the Nova Scotia legislature from one seat (her own) to three.[48] In New Brunswick, NDP leader Elizabeth Weir increased her party's seat count from zero to one, when she won her home constituency in Saint John.[49]

Yet the patterns that tend to stick in our minds go in the opposite direction. Rita Johnston's brief tenure as Social Credit leader and premier in British Columbia saw that party's seat count drop from 47 to 7 in the 1991 provincial elections, with an equally steep drop-off in the popular vote.[50] When Nancy MacBeth served as leader of the Alberta Liberals from 1998 to 2001, the party slipped from 18 seats in the provincial legislature to only seven.[51] Ginny Hasselfield's time as leader of the Manitoba Liberals saw major splits in that party's three-member caucus.[52] Elizabeth Weir was succeeded as NDP leader in New Brunswick by Allison Brewer, who resigned after the party's popular vote plummeted and the NDP seat count returned to zero in the 2006 provincial elections.[53]

Even more memorable than the inability of female politicians to turn around the depressed fortunes of weak parties, were cases in which a woman won the leadership of a competitive party—and then, despite poll results suggesting victory was within reach, her party lost the next election. Regrettably for the cause of women in Canadian politics, one such scenario unfolded in the country's most populous province. Lyn McLeod, who had a successful career as a school trustee and provincial legislator from Thunder Bay, became leader of the Ontario Liberals in 1992, when Bob Rae's NDP government held office. McLeod was widely expected to become the province's next premier, but instead wound up as Opposition leader during the early years of Mike Harris' Conservative government.[54]

These examples of women leading weak parties, as well as McLeod's experience of losing a crucial election at the helm of a competitive organization, seem to dominate our memories. As a result, we recall hardly any good news about women's electoral triumphs. In a fascinating case of selective retention disorder on a national scale, we almost entirely forget about successful female politicians who contested top office and actually held powerful positions at the provincial, territorial, and local levels. These winners include Prince Edward Island premier Catherine Callbeck, Northwest Territories government leader Nellie Cournoyea, Yukon government head Pat Duncan, and Mississauga mayor Hazel McCallion.

Shortly after Callbeck became Liberal leader in PEI in 1993, her party captured every seat except one in the provincial legislature, meaning she led a nearly wall-to-wall majority government. The irony is that Callbeck's accomplishment was overshadowed in the spring of 1993 by Brian Mulroney's resignation as federal Conservative leader, and all the hoopla surrounding Kim Campbell's rough time as his successor.

In the territories, Cournoyea became legislative leader in the Northwest Territories in 1991, and was the first aboriginal woman in Canada to hold a political executive post. Duncan led the Yukon Liberals to victory in 2000. At the municipal level, McCallion continues a long tradition of outspoken women mayors going back to Charlotte Whitton in Ottawa during the 1950s. Known as a no-nonsense local politician, McCallion serves as the mayor of Canada's sixth-largest city. She presides over a Mississauga city council of 11 members representing a population of more than 700,000 residents, and has been consistently elected and re-elected by large margins since 1978. In the 2006 municipal elections, she garnered 91 percent of the popular vote.

Parallel with our disconcerting tendency to associate political women with electoral loss is the disparate treatment accorded to men. After all, many Canadian men have led their parties to doom and gloom results. Yet never does the subsequent public consensus fixate on men as losers. Thinking back to major fizzles involving men on top, we can recall Ujjal Dosanjh's term as leader of the BC NDP, when that party slid from 39 to 2 seats in the 2001 provincial elections.[55] Dosanjh was later courted for a federal Liberal nomination, switched parties and levels of government, and went on to serve in Paul Martin's cabinet as minister of health. No negative halo is detectable in his trajectory, despite the fact that Dosanjh effectively deserted the party he'd left decimated in BC.

As was the case with Rita Johnston and Kim Campbell, Dosanjh became leader of a governing party that was on its way out. My point is not that parties falter from time to time, but rather that we respond to the waves of loss and triumph differently depending on a leader's gender. In the case of men, there are enough of them who win elections that we see no need to obsess over the ones who lose. In fact, our practice is often to offer solace, consolation, and convenient landing pads for men in pain. The contrast between Dosanjh's fate and that of his fellow British Columbian is stark and clear: since Kim Campbell resigned as Progressive Conservative leader following the 1993 federal election, she has consistently lived and worked outside the country, and has not to my knowledge been offered any convenient landing pads in Canadian electoral politics.

The dark shadows cast by the experiences of McLaughlin, McDonough, and Campbell at the federal level, and by patterns at the provincial level whereby women have led weak parties or, in McLeod's case, lost an election at the helm of a competitive one, continue to exert ripple effects. They reinforce the *discomfort equation* by creating an additional source of unease; namely, that female leaders "cause" their parties to fail. And once women on top are blamed for washout debacles and portrayed as political losers, new recruits become even harder to find.

It's worth asking in light of this background whether Canadian women should stop contesting top posts in weak parties. Paying closer attention to the consequences of uncompetitive party leadership doesn't mean no individuals will put themselves forward for such positions. Nor does it remove the possibility that some weak parties might become highly competitive. The purpose of posing the question is simply to ask how we might sever the damaging thought associations we've created.

During the early postwar years, party recruiters tended to place women candidates in lost-cause constituencies. This created an impression that female candidates could not win—which became an indefensible view once more of them contested promising seats, and did as well as or better than men from the same parties. More recently, women's positions as leaders of marginal parties have lent credence to the view that they depressed or even destroyed party fortunes—when, on closer inspection, it's fair to ask what human being in similar circumstances could have produced better results.

At its heart, the *women plus power equals discomfort* equation teaches us not to be naïve. Winning a competitive party leadership race is extremely difficult for both men and women, and women face profound unease over how they should perform on that particular stage. As we've seen, aggressive interventions draw media attention but, at the same time, conflict with prevailing expectations about how women should act. Quieter styles are widely ignored, and become largely invisible in a sea of commentary about the attention-grabbers. Clearly, the odds of winning a low-stakes position far exceed the chances of succeeding in a high-stakes environment, so it's not hard to understand why most women leaders in Canadian parties won in the former context. Yet the costs of this pattern are far from negligible.

As if these leadership style difficulties were not dicey enough, there's a hornet's nest of conflicting judgments about the proper personal characteristics of women in Canadian politics. We turn our attention to them in Chapter 3.

Notes

1. Adams reports this decline occurred between 1992 and 2000. Michael Adams, *Fire and Ice: The United States, Canada and the Myth of Converging Values* (Toronto: Penguin, 2003), 51. See also Neil Nevitte, *The Decline of Deference: Canadian Value Change in Cross-National Perspective* (Peterborough: Broadview, 1996).

2. That being said, it's not clear that successful women and men differ all that much in their leadership styles. See Carol Hymowitz, "Women Internalize Bias: Study," *The Globe and Mail* (28 October 2005), C2; and Barbara Kellerman and Deborah Rhode, eds., *Women and Leadership: The State of Play and Strategies for Change* (San Francisco: Jossey-Bass, 2007).

3. On the argument that parliamentary systems are more welcoming toward women than presidential ones, and that the US is a particularly difficult case, see Ann Gordon, "A Woman in the White House? Never say never," in Lori Cox Han and Caroline Heldman, eds., *Rethinking Madam President* (Boulder, Colorado: Lynne Rienner, 2007), 186–188.

4. See Brian Milner, "Poll Finds Men Preferred as Boss," *The Globe and Mail* (27 March 1996).

5. *Women in Canada 2000: A Gender-Based Statistical Report* (Ottawa: Statistics Canada, 2000).

6. See executive search data reported in Wallace Immen, "Women in Top Positions on the Decline," *The Globe and Mail* (16 January 2008), C2.

7. Meredith Conroy, "Political Parties: Advancing a Masculine Ideal," in Han and Heldman, eds., *Rethinking Madam President*, 141.

8. *The Random House Dictionary of the English Language* (New York: Random House, 1971), 814.

9. Virginia Valian, *Why So Slow? The Advancement of Women* (Cambridge: MIT Press, 1998), 11.

10. Pippa Norris, "Introduction: Women, Media, and Politics," in Pippa Norris, ed., *Women, Media, and Politics* (New York: Oxford University Press, 1997), 2. Theories of framing draw heavily on the work of sociologists Erving Goffman and Todd Gitlin.

11. David Niven, "Gender Bias? Media Coverage of Women and Men in Congress," in Sue Tolleson-Rinehart and Jyl J. Josephson, eds., *Gender and American Politics: Women, Men, and the Political Process* (Armonk, NY: Sharpe, 2005), 265, 278.

12. Valian, *Why So Slow?* 21.

13. Norris, "Introduction," 8, 9.

14. Valian, *Why So Slow?* 129, 133, 295.

15. Valian, *Why So Slow?* 136.

16. Among the most compelling empirical studies in this area is Kristyn A. Scott and Douglas J. Brown, "Female First, Leader Second? Gender Bias in the Encoding of Leadership Behavior," *Organizational Behavior and Human Decision Processes* 101 (2006), 230–242. See also Lisa Belkin, "Why Women Just Can't Win at Work," *The Globe and Mail* (7 November 2007), C7.

17. Caroline Heldman, "Cultural Barriers to a Female President in the United States," in Han and Heldman, eds., *Rethinking Madam President*, 21, 22.

18. Niven, "Gender Bias," 276.

19. See Louise Carbert, *Rural Women's Leadership in Atlantic Canada: First Hand Perspectives on Local Public Life and Participation in Electoral Politics* (Toronto: University of Toronto Press, 2006); Elizabeth Goodyear-Grant, "Crafting a Public Image: Women MPs and the Dynamics of Media Coverage," in Sylvia Bashevkin, ed., *Opening Doors Wider: Women's Political Engagement in Canada* (Vancouver: UBC Press, 2009), 147–66.

20. See Louise Carbert, "Are Cities More Congenial? Tracking the Rural Deficit of Women in the House of Commons," in Bashevkin, ed., *Opening Doors Wider*, 70–90.

21. On the crucial role of ambition in public careers, see Jennifer L. Lawless and Richard L. Fox, *It Takes a Candidate: Why Women Don't Run for Office* (Cambridge: Cambridge University Press, 2005).

22. See Rosemary Brown, *Being Brown: A Very Public Life* (Toronto: Random House, 1989), 102–104; Audrey McLaughlin with Rick Archbold, *A Woman's Place: My Life and Politics* (Toronto: Macfarlane, Walter and Ross, 1992), 7, 13.

23. John Ibbitson, "Brown's No Fool—This Relationship is Still Special," *The Globe and Mail* (31 July 2007), A11.

24. Crosbie as quoted in Sheila Copps, *Nobody's Baby: A Survival Guide to Politics* (Toronto: Deneau, 1986), 169.

25. Brian Gable's cartoon was published in *The Globe and Mail* on 17 January 1990.

26. Joan Bryden, "Liberals Wonder if Copps Bubble has Been Burst," *The Toronto Star* (28 April 1990).

27. McLaughlin, *A Woman's Place*, 57, 58.

28. McLaughlin, *A Woman's Place*, 22–23.

29. Joanna Everitt and Elisabeth Gidengil, "Tough Talk: How Television News Covers Male and Female Leaders of Canadian Political Parties," in Manon Tremblay and Linda Trimble, eds., *Women and Electoral Politics in Canada* (Toronto: Oxford University Press, 2003), 201. See also Elisabeth Gidengil and Joanna Everitt, "Conventional

Coverage/ Unconventional Politicians: Gender and Media Coverage of Canadian Leaders' Debates, 1993, 1997, 2000," *Canadian Journal of Political Science* 36:3 (July-August 2003), 559–577.

30. Everitt and Gidengil, "Tough Talk," 201.

31. Everitt and Gidengil, "Tough Talk," 204.

32. Everitt and Gidengil, "Tough Talk," 198.

33. These terms are drawn from a *Toronto Sun* headline and a CTV report, as quoted in David McLaughlin, *Poisoned Chalice: The Last Campaign of the Progressive Conservative Party?* (Toronto: Dundurn, 1994), 233.

34. Everitt and Gidengil, "Tough Talk," 208.

35. McLaughlin, *Poisoned Chalice*, 230.

36. See McLaughlin, *Poisoned Chalice*, 230.

37. Gidengil and Everitt, "Conventional Coverage/Unconventional Politicians," 561.

38. Niven, "Gender Bias," 276.

39. Linda Trimble, "Who Framed Belinda Stronach? National Newspaper Coverage of the Conservative Party of Canada's 2004 Leadership Race," paper presented at Canadian Political Science Association meetings, University of Western Ontario, 2005, 7.

40. Linda Trimble and Jane Arscott, *Still Counting: Women in Politics Across Canada* (Peterborough: Broadview, 2003), 98–99.

41. See Trimble and Arscott, *Still Counting*, 83. In the second volume of his memoirs, Jean Chrétien claimed more Canadians believed Elvis Presley was still alive in 1993 than approved of Brian Mulroney's performance as prime minister. See Jean Chrétien, *My Years as Prime Minister* (Toronto: Random House, 2007).

42. Kim Campbell, *Time and Chance: The Political Memoirs of Canada's First Woman Prime Minister* (Toronto: Doubleday, 1996), 263.

43. See http://en.wikipedia.org/wiki/Parti_social-d%C3%A9 mocratique, consulted 20 September 2007.

44. See http://en.wikipedia.org/wiki/New_Democratic_Party_ of_British_Columbia, consulted 20 September 2007.

45. See http://en.wikipedia.org/wiki/Pam_Barrett, consulted 24 September 2007.
46. See http://en.wikipedia.org/wiki/Lynda_Haverstock, consulted 20 September 2007.
47. See http://en.wikipedia.org/wiki/Sharon_Carstairs, consulted 24 September 2007.
48. See http://en.wikipedia.org/wiki/New_Democratic_Party_%28Nova_Scotia%29#Alexa_McDonough, consulted 20 September 2007.
49. See http://en.wikipedia.org/wiki/Elizabeth_Weir, consulted 20 September 2007.
50. See http://en.wikipedia.org/wiki/British_Columbia_general_election%2C_1991, consulted 20 September 2007.
51. See http://en.wikipedia.org/wiki/Nancy_MacBeth, consulted 20 September 2007.
52. See http://en.wikipedia.org/wiki/Manitoba_Liberal_Party, consulted 24 September 2007.
53. See http://en.wikipedia.org/wiki/Allison_Brewer, consulted 20 September 2007.
54. A parallel case unfolded in Newfoundland in the mid-1990s, when Lynn Verge became leader of the provincial Conservatives at a time when that party was expected to win the next election. Instead, Liberal leader Brian Tobin became premier of the province following the 1996 elections. See http://en.wikipedia.org/wiki/Lyn_McLeod, consulted 20 September 2007.
55. See http://en.wikipedia.org/wiki/British_Columbia_general_election%2C_2001, consulted 20 September 2007.

3

Plus-perfect Figures

Women who've sought top political posts in Canada are nearly as diverse as the 52 percent of the country's population who are female. Some have been on the young side of the average, like Sheila Copps when she sought the Ontario Liberal leadership in 1982. Others were somewhat older, notably Pauline Marois when she became Parti Québécois (PQ) chief in 2007. A number grew up in affluent families in metropolitan areas, like 2004 Conservative leadership candidate Belinda Stronach. Others came from modest rural circumstances, including 1976 Progressive Conservative candidate Flora MacDonald. A few came to Canada as immigrants, including 1975 NDP contender Rosemary Brown. Kim Campbell had blond hair; others including Flora MacDonald and BC NDP leader Joy Macphail were redheads; and most were brunettes. Some, including Audrey McLaughlin, spoke in quiet cadences, while others (including Copps and Campbell) expressed themselves using more emphatic and forthright styles.

The intriguing similarity among all these varied politicians was not that each had distinctive personal characteristics, nor that each faced sustained scrutiny of her suitability for top public office. In a democratic society, after all, we expect candidates who seek positions of responsibility to come from disparate backgrounds, and to be evaluated, assessed, and considered rather than simply foisted on a passive citizenry. What's striking is that so many discussions about each of these individuals focused on detailed assessments of their personal characteristics—especially age, appearance, and speaking style.

Ironically, research in Canada, the United States, and elsewhere shows that as a group, female office-holders receive less media attention than do their male counterparts. Yet at the same time, much of the coverage women do attract focuses on personal style and private life matters rather than on public policy views.[1] This ongoing fixation with matters unrelated to political substance effectively converts women politicians into physical commodities, treated as if they are involuntary contestants on an extended, and very high-stakes, makeover show. Within this strange public spectacle, very few demographic characteristics, visual images, or communications styles are viewed as acceptable in their unvarnished (or pre-makeover) form. Instead, various personal characteristics are placed under a microscope, subjected to close evaluative scrutiny, and deemed, like a suit that never fits, in need of various alterations.

Unlike the classic tale of "Goldilocks and the Three Bears," in which eventually the golden-haired young girl found a bed that felt good and a porridge temperature that was just right, political women in Canada can't seem to find ages, clothes, or speaking styles that correspond with what we as the assessors deem appropriate. This situation parallels the story presented in Chapter 2, in which dissections of the leadership styles of female politicians found both assertive and consensual approaches to be lacking, meaning women in public life had a hard time finding appropriate ways to project their authoritative roles.

The remarkable aspect of the style-based scrutiny discussed below is that for the most part, it's been not at all subtle. I was reminded of just how striking this treatment can be early one Saturday morning, while flipping through the Life section of *The Globe and Mail*. Now, you might ask, isn't that part of the paper supposed to be all about style? Well, yes, it is, and I confess upfront to a certain fondness for the inventive recipes, home décor tips, and gardening advice offered each week.

But what struck my eye this particular Saturday was a column by Karen von Hahn, titled "Hillary needs to channel her inner beeyatch." It began by noting that a 2007 public opinion poll in the United States had found 11 percent of Americans "were 'uncomfortable' with voting for a woman" for president. Von Hahn continued as follows: "When I read that, I was amazed. Hillary is a woman? Who'd have thought that under those beige pantsuits so shapeless they would meet with Taliban approval there lurks a real, live female?"

Bingo, I thought. A woman columnist in a Canadian national newspaper of record not only has determined she's on a first-name basis with a respected US Senator and leading Democratic party presidential candidate, but also has decided she's got spare ink to spill over trouser tailoring. But then things got even more interesting. It turns out that this writer wanted to explain why she agreed with survey respondents who saw Clinton as dishonest and untrustworthy. Quoting von Hahn: "Of course we want to see a woman in the White House. But how can we trust her if she acts like a eunuch?...Where are the mercurial, impetuous flashes of passion that, as any woman knows, are driving the rest of us half-insane? ... Here is my prescription for Hillary Clinton: Stop campaigning like you've been neutered and have the balls to run like a real girl."

And what did this last bit of advice mean? Well, it boiled down to preventing "her philandering Bill" from stealing the limelight at public events (by teaching him to adopt the model of Denis Thatcher as a properly deferential political husband), and avoiding the "sexless, Talbot-clad wonk" look she'd thus far projected. How to remedy this last problem? Aha, go shopping with pal Oscar de la Renta—obviously at a store other than Talbot's. Once the ex-president was on an appropriately short leash and his wife was attired in the proper clothes, von Hahn asserted, Candidate Clinton could "stand up straight and show us your claws and…your cleavage."[2]

So, I wondered, is that all that's required for a woman to be taken seriously in politics? Step one, show more hot emotion. Step two, take lessons in taming one's husband. Step three, wear sexy clothes that showcase a curvy bosom.

Would that things were all so simple. We know from the research findings presented in Chapter 2 that displaying claws in public does not necessarily work to the advantage of female politicians. An assertive public demeanour, as Kim Campbell demonstrated in 1993, can be portrayed as combative and hyper-masculine—even if men in the same forum behave more aggressively. The prospects for husband-taming? Chapter 4 probes the tempestuous realm of love and romance. Suffice it to say here that such terrain is exceedingly fraught with danger for political women, particularly those who are not in heterosexual marriages. If we use Canadian evidence to draw lessons for a US politician, in fact, it would appear that Hillary Clinton made a reasonable career choice in remaining married to her husband, since single and divorced women in politics seem to draw more scrutiny than their married counterparts.

The clothes to wear, though. Now there's an issue of substance. It has garnered enormous attention since Canada's first female MP, Agnes Macphail, took her seat in the House of Commons in 1921. Macphail's entry to Parliament was headline news in the social pages of the nation's newspapers, which devoted considerable attention to her hat, gloves, and dress. All were found wanting, as severe, worn out, unfashionable, and downright dowdy.[3]

A close reading of media accounts about women politicians since Macphail's time shows the emphasis on physical appearances, and on plus-perfect expectations of them, has continued for close to 90 years. These portrayals not only underline an ongoing discomfort with the presence of females in the traditionally male-dominated enclave of politics; they also give free rein to our willingness to obsessively dissect, criticize, and ultimately try to reformat women's personal attributes. By implication, style-based discussions of female politicians in the media offer us as readers, viewers, and listeners a parallel licence—indeed, sustained encouragement—from the official purveyors of political analysis to do more of the same. The upshot is that women's status as deviant outsiders in the political realm is consistently confirmed, as they are consigned to the "lightweight" status of style items in the country's news media and, as we mimic that treatment, in our own private conversations.

Just as the phrase "women on top" usually evokes a perfectly toned sexual image, in which the female we conjure up is a flawless model of both physical beauty and human responsiveness, the model political woman is expected to meet the same unrealistic standards. If the sexual image shows a thin, lithe, and energetic body, below an attractive face that is not tired, bored, or distracted, so too does the political image demand similarly exacting criteria.

In Canada, we've come to believe women in public life should be thin, mature, well dressed, and well coiffed, and must speak with well-modulated voices. Obviously, each of these characteristics is entirely subjective. What is thin in our own estimation? Mature, meaning older than 22 but not too old? Well dressed, meaning stylish is preferable to frumpy, but just how stylish? Hair that's clean and neat, but not so attractive that it raises the question of whether Woman X has a brain underneath? A voice that's resonant and clear, but not so authoritative that it's—heaven forbid—too powerful?

Given that one person's tasteful wardrobe is another's recidivist fashion crime, it is not surprising that we're confused by the barrage of personal style messages about women in politics. My point in this chapter is very consciously not to prescribe a one-size-fits-all age, clothes, hair, or voice remedy for the courageous individuals who seek to serve us in public life. It would be presumptuous to assume that all politicians, whether male or female, should look, dress, or speak the same way, just as it would be ridiculous to propose that all bankers, social workers, or professors should do so either.

Rather, the purpose of this discussion is to shed light on the obscuring of women's contributions to the substance of policy debate, which results from their long-term presence in the crosshairs of media style mavens. Evaluations of female politicians that employ a plus-perfect metric—and therefore find them wanting—ensure we as citizens face a barrage of commentary about supposed personal flaws and shortcomings. What gets lost in the process is the opportunity not only to ask whether style matters to democratic life, but also to comprehend female politicians as rightful public participants, who hold meaningful ideas and beliefs about our local communities, our country, and the larger world.

Facing the Demographic Juggernaut

Statistics Canada reported recently that approximately 60 percent of adults in this country are either overweight or obese.[4] Government data also show the country's population is aging rapidly, despite the ongoing influx of immigrants to large cities.[5] My own observations of the House of Commons as well as provincial legislatures and city council chambers offer a far from scientifically rigorous sample, but they do confirm parallels between these demographic trends and what's visible from the visitor's gallery.

In particular, I've noticed that lots of elected officials are haggard-looking middle-aged and older men, and that many of them wear nondescript dark suits—apparently to help mask the effects of too many lunches, cocktail parties, and dinners on the rubber-chicken-and-chocolate-mousse circuit. Aging affects all of us, but weight gain and loss of sleep due to uncontrollable hours of work seem to be particular occupational hazards for politicians. In order to meet their constituents and contributors, they're expected to spend long hours at public receptions and other events. Their bodies eventually show the results, just as bruised jaws and broken noses often characterize hockey players who play a spirited game on the ice.

Since the paunchy middles and tired faces of male politicians have become more or less *de rigueur* fixtures in legislatures and city councils, they elicit about as much public attention as bandages on goalies. We almost never hear people say that Mr. X MP or Mr. Y councillor is a worn-out, over-ripe politico who needs to find a new tailor.

By way of contrast, we frequently get an earful about the flawed personal features of women in public life. Since the latter are so few relative both to men politicians and to women in the general public, their individual characteristics are far more likely to be noticed, scrutinized, and remarked upon. Moreover, little mercy or forgiveness is extended to women politicians who show the effects of their occupational experiences. In fact, as I discuss later on in this chapter, they are unable to arrive at work, day after day, wearing clothes equally shapeless as those worn by their male colleagues. Karen von Hahn's comments quoted earlier about Hillary Clinton show exactly what happens when a woman politician appears regularly in public in pantsuits similar to those worn by men: she risks being condemned as a dowdy, "sexless, Talbot-clad wonk." Not a pretty piece of spin.

Age is another problem for political women. Somehow, unlike Goldilocks finding suitable food and lodging at the bears' house, they can't seem to attain the "just right" age. Some are accused of being too young. Unlike men who are bold, energetic high-flyers if they move up quickly in their 20s or 30s, young women with equivalent levels of ambition are tagged as inexperienced and over-zealous, and risky bets for public leadership.

The classic Canadian case of the too-young woman was Sheila Copps in the 1982 race to lead the Ontario Liberals. As a 28-year-old with less than one year of experience as the provincial member for Hamilton Centre, Copps declared her candidacy in November 1981 for the party's top post.

You would have thought all hell had broken loose. Copps was certainly a maverick, having announced that she would press independently to have protection from discrimination on the basis of sexual orientation included in the provincial Human Rights Code. One Conservative cabinet minister told her on the floor of the legislature that she was better-looking than a woman who had retired some time earlier from the Liberal caucus. Another Tory MPP urged her to "go back to the kitchen." Copps refused to suffer their comments in silence, and wrote publicly about what she later came to see as a lingering "men's-club mentality" at Queen's Park.[6]

This was obviously all too much for the top politicos in Canada's largest city. Hugh Winsor, then working for *The Globe and Mail* at Queen's Park, posed the suitability question directly in a December 1981 column. In his words, "The question facing the delegates of the OLP leadership convention when they gather here next February is simple. Will the voters of Ontario in 1985 choose a government led by a 32-year-old woman, albeit an attractive, intelligent one?" Winsor went on to describe the personal style of Ms. Copps, whom he referred to in his column as "Sheila," as "brash, gutsy, impudent, even impatient."[7] Readers were not treated to a parallel assessment of the personality traits of David Peterson or the other three male candidates for the OLP leadership, perhaps because the very traits identified in Winsor's list would have been deemed acceptable, even downright attractive, in a man.

Delegates to the Liberal leadership convention echoed Winsor's query, buzzing about with concerns for whether "Ontario will vote for a woman," "…a 29-year-old woman" or "…a 29-year-old single woman." The fact that Bob Rae was all of 33 years old when he became Ontario NDP leader—also in 1982—seemed entirely irrelevant to these musings about Sheila Copps. And, one year later, the fact that Brian Mulroney became leader of the federal Progressive Conservatives without ever having served a day in elective public office was similarly ignored.

Unfortunately, experience for women politicians offers no antidote to this problem. It's possible to be not only too old, but also too veteran. My sharpest awakening to this reality came in response to former Parti Québécois cabinet minister Pauline Marois's efforts in 2005 and 2007 to win that party's top position. In 2005, at the age of 56, she campaigned to succeed then 68-year-old PQ leader

Bernard Landry. As *La Presse* columnist Lysiane Gagnon observed, Marois was portrayed as having "been around for so long that people see her as a has-been."[8] Marois had indeed held 11 different government portfolios since entering politics in the early 1980s, and was responsible for introducing innovative pay equity and universal five-dollar-a-day child-care programs in Quebec.

Marois's main opponent in the 2005 race was 39-year-old André Boisclair, who'd served briefly as a junior PQ cabinet minister. During the course of that leadership campaign, Boisclair admitted he had used cocaine while an MNA and cabinet minister.[9] This statement, alongside an earlier public declaration of his homosexuality, seemed only to strengthen Boisclair's credentials as a fresh, energetic, and lively politician. As Lysiane Gagnon correctly predicted before the PQ leadership vote, Boisclair "might end up winning the race because he is handsome, smart and fit, and because he projects an image of youth in a party of aging baby boomers."

Marois ended up more than 20 percentage points behind on the one and only PQ leadership ballot, and lost the 2005 race. Yet Boisclair stumbled badly as leader, to the point that the PQ placed behind both the Liberal and upstart Action Démocratique du Québec (ADQ) parties in the March 2007 Quebec elections. Once he resigned the position that May, Marois announced for the third time that she would run for the top job in the PQ, and won by acclamation.

Boisclair's implosion was not the first for a man in politics, nor will it be the last. Consistent with my argument in Chapter 2, however, political observers did not tag all men as losers because of one man's debacle. Moreover, the likely cause of Boisclair's poor showing—namely, a lack of solid judgment that generally comes from years of legislative and cabinet experience—did not universally highlight Marois's strengths. The contrast between the content of Lysiane Gagnon's columns, and demeaning comments about the age and experience of Pauline Marois that popped up elsewhere in the Canadian press, was hard to miss.

One particularly stunning example of this pattern appeared in a *Globe and Mail* column by Jeffrey Simpson, titled "The PQ has a funny way of 'renewing' its leadership." It described Marois as "a comforting, comfortable, almost grandmotherly figure who had given no offence." Simpson suggested she was so old, so tired, and so much "yesterday's woman" that "If Ms. Marois's ascension represents 'renewal,' and all those other buzz words so favoured by parties in the dumps, then the federal Liberals should bring back Herb Gray."[10]

As a postscript to that dismissive commentary, permit me to append the following: In 2007, Marois was 58 years old, while Gray was 76. That means women wither so rapidly in Jeffrey Simpson's calculus that they gain nearly 20 years over men by middle age. This view of women's biological ages far eclipsing those of men contradicts a fundamental cornerstone of actuarial research, which is that men age much faster than women. Actuarial projections, in fact, explain why on average women in middle age pay far lower life insurance premiums than do men of the same age.

You might well ask: How can respected political columnists like Simpson and Winsor get away with promulgating such biased perspectives about the too-old or too-young features of female politicians? I've often asked myself the same question, and offer some suggestions for fixing their wagons in Chapter 6.

In the meantime, let me suggest that the analytic edge offered in Lysiane Gagnon's treatment of PQ leadership races remains the exception rather than the rule. For other journalists, facts are conveniently shielded so as not to get in the way of a good crack at Pauline Marois, Sheila Copps, or their female colleagues. At its heart, the *women plus power equals discomfort* equation means that fairness, reason, and logic are easily trumped by their opposites— including when assessing basic personal characteristics such as the age of women leaders.

Dressing for Success

We can find at least as profound a sense of unease in discussions about physical appearance. Unlike male politicos, who face limited options in clothing and hair, females have lots of choices. The problem, according to conventional wisdom, is they can't seem to get the possibilities sorted out properly.

One woman's sense of tasteful, appropriate clothing can be publicly deemed a fashion disaster, as we saw earlier with columnist Karen von Hahn's verdict on Hillary Clinton's trousers. Dressing very well is even more of a high-wire act. Designer labels can set off flashing lights on the discomfort meter because they arouse deeply embedded tensions about social class. After all, who does Ms. X think she is, dressed like that? Where did she get the money to buy those clothes? Decisions by US Republicans to invest heavily in the campaign clothing worn by 2008 vice-presidential nominee Sarah Palin and members of her family set off precisely this sort of discomfort.

Even getting decently coiffed remains a serious challenge. News outlets in the United States devoted so much attention to Hillary Clinton's hair that the New York senator once commented, "If I want to knock a story off the front page, I just change my hairstyle."[11] We've all heard about the importance of visual images to celebrity photographs, television, and Internet coverage, which means hair that is not reasonably stylish tends to make anyone who appears regularly in the media—including politicians—look frumpy and outdated. At the other end of the spectrum, however, sporting au courant and otherwise well-arranged hair can be a liability as well, because it leads commentators to wonder if the brain under the mane is simple, shallow, or otherwise deficient in the hard matter department.

To wit, let's consider the attractive long hair of Conservative MP Rona Ambrose, who was appointed to Stephen Harper's first cabinet in 2006 as minister of the environment. Ambrose's appearance was deemed so notable by *Maclean's* that an article about her in an issue on the new Tory government was titled "The Beauty."[12] What she looked like was briefly more newsworthy than the fact that Harper and his policy advisors had no idea what to do about climate change and other pressing environmental issues. The next wrinkle in the story unfortunately set up Ambrose to take the fall for this policy gap: as criticism piled up from the opposition, interest groups, and the public on the lack of federal action, Harper demoted Ambrose from his front-bench cabinet, assigning her to the far less visible intergovernmental affairs portfolio, and little more was heard about the former environment minister or her hair.

If being too glamorous doesn't work in Ottawa, neither does being too plain. And sometimes the dissection process is so complicated that a single individual may draw widely varying comments during the course of one career.[13] Overall, women from Atlantic Canada who enter federal politics seem to face the harshest image-based commentary from reporters as well as fellow politicians. This may result from the different style norms prevailing in central Canada, notably Ottawa, versus those of the provinces east of Quebec.

Among the most memorable press accounts that suggested political women did not know how to present themselves in a polished way were early stories about Cape Breton native Flora MacDonald, and more recent ones about former Saint John mayor Elsie Wayne. In fact, in her study of why so few female politicians are active in Eastern Canada, Louise Carbert concluded that the mocking by Ottawa MPs and journalists of Wayne's sweater wardrobe strongly discouraged potential federal candidates from that region. Wayne was mocked in 2003 by Liberal defence minister John McCallum, after she asked a question in Parliament about reflective markings on Canadian armoured vehicles. McCallum's reply, on a day when Wayne wore a sequined sweater in the House of Commons, was: "It has been suggested that if our soldiers were to wear the dress of the honourable member, that they would be very well identified."[14] According to Carbert's research, few women from Eastern Canada were willing to become live cadavers, ready to undergo ongoing, detailed style autopsies in the nation's capital.[15]

Wayne's experiences paralleled those of Nova Scotia MP Alexa McDonough. During the time she served as federal NDP leader, a story appeared in the *Ottawa Citizen* featuring a large photo above the headline, "Alexa McDonough, Call your dry-cleaner."[16] Looking back on her memories of this account in a conversation with Queen's University political scientist Elizabeth Goodyear-Grant, McDonough argued that the story behind the caption was that she had, in one week, worn the same dress to two public events. McDonough posed the obvious question: "Could you imagine a story with the following headline: Jean Chrétien wears same suit twice in one week? No man has ten suits, and no one expects him to, but a woman is supposed to have a closet full of clothes."[17]

If they want to avoid allegations of being under-dressed for public life, women politicians risk being accused of being too well-dressed. Arguably the most racially charged depiction of this type affected the NDP's Rosemary Brown, an immigrant from Jamaica who first won her Vancouver-area seat in the BC legislature in 1972. Brown's decision to seek the top post in the federal party in 1975 coincided with the rise of second-wave feminism—and with demands from Brown and many others that women's political equality belonged on the local, provincial, and national public agendas.

Brown's leadership bid was significant not only because it marked the first competitive effort by a woman to win the leadership of a major federal party; the campaign remains important and unique because Brown's platform was assertively feminist, explicitly socialist, and unabashedly anti-racist. What's more, she came close enough to defeating insider candidate Ed Broadbent that her candidacy generated "real apprehension among the party establishment."[18]

Very few confident, outspoken, high-profile, and radical black women were active at the time in Canadian politics. Brown's ability to take on the NDP leadership race, and to compete with Broadbent and three other male candidates through four rounds of convention voting, was widely noticed by the public, the media, and other politicians. What seemed to particularly rankle commentators, though, was Brown's polished appearance. She was frequently described in the press as an elegant, eloquent, well-dressed black woman who lived in Vancouver's wealthy Point Grey neighbourhood, and who held an extensive portfolio of private stocks as well as real estate in the Gulf Islands.[19]

This unsettling portrayal of Brown as a stylish left-wing politician reflected a larger unease with how, as a former social worker and current member of the BC legislature, she could afford to look so good. As I argue in Chapter 4, the romantic (and, by implication, financial) entanglements of women in Canadian public life never cease to fascinate. In 1975, reporters were quick to assure those who followed the NDP race that candidate Brown was married to an American-born psychiatrist, Bill Brown, whose flourishing practice underwrote the couple's lifestyle.

Some readers may wave off this example, and dismiss the style treatment of Rosemary Brown as (pardon my pun) old hat. That's particularly likely if you were born since 1975, and can't imagine how outdated stereotypes from more than 30 years ago could possibly hold any resonance today. Who, you might ask, really cares how a woman politician pays for her wardrobe? Perhaps she shops at outlet malls. Or sews her own clothes. Maybe she won the lottery. Basically, who cares?

For each reader who poses that question, allow me to once again introduce Pauline Marois. When she ran unsuccessfully for the PQ's top post against André Boisclair in 2005, Marois was accused of dressing too well for the prospective leader of a centre-left party. In writing about this subject, journalist Lysiane Gagnon summarized the critical talk as follows: "Much was made of Ms. Marois's costly clothes, leading to accusations that she's a haughty 'bourgeoise' (something that her social-worker speaking style and behaviour totally belie). Yet nobody seems to mind that Mr. Boisclair has his suits cut by trendy designer Philippe Dubuc." Gagnon went on to point out that Mr. Boisclair came from an upper-middle-class family background, while "Ms. Marois's father owned a gas station."[20]

Although it was devoid of a racial overlay, much of the anxiety about Marois came from similar sources as for Brown: if she came from a family of modest means (parallel with Brown's origins as an immigrant from the Caribbean) and had worked for years as a member of the Quebec National Assembly (as Brown had served in the BC legislature) then how did she pay for nice clothes? Again, the trusty explanation drew on the background of Marois's husband, Claude Blanchet who, as Gagnon noted, "made money decades ago in real estate."[21] Blanchet went on to serve as president of Quebec's public investment fund, known as the Société générale de financement, but resigned from that position in 2003.

In short, insecurities that we confront in Canada about the clothing worn by women politicians tends to reflect deeper anxieties concerning wealth and social class. But this same unease is profoundly entangled as well with questions about authenticity, namely: Are well-dressed women the *real* source of their own seeming affluence, or is someone else footing the bill? The conclusion we're left to draw about Rosemary Brown and Pauline Marois is this: if their husbands made it possible for them to dress and otherwise live so well, then neither was authentically rich. Both were recipients of spousal largesse, plain and simple.

Now spousal largesse can work in both directions, as anyone who follows family income data can discern. In growing numbers of households in Canada and elsewhere, women are the major, and sometimes the only, breadwinner. Outside this country, we know prominent male politicians who have been heavily supported financially by their wives' incomes, including Bill Clinton while he was governor of Arkansas and later US president, and Tony

Blair when he was an MP and later British prime minister. That's because both Hillary Rodham Clinton and Cherie (Booth) Blair built up lucrative legal practices and landed major book deals that far eclipsed what their husbands earned as political executives.

The boundaries of financial support also extend to parents. We know, for example, that Pierre Trudeau inherited a considerable family fortune and had very limited earned income of his own—he started his first regular job in his late forties. Yet it's hard to recall much in the way of innuendo suggesting Trudeau was at all inauthentic, even though he wore stylish suits, flowers in his lapel, dashing hats, sweeping capes, and so on, not to mention that he drove an antique Mercedes-Benz convertible and lived in an art deco mansion in Westmount—most of it thanks to his family wealth. Because well-turned-out men like Trudeau are seen as natural inhabitants of the political realm, their personal style comes off as bold and daring, full of flair and vigour, rather than serving as a target for loaded questions about authenticity and legitimacy.

For women in public life, personal attractiveness provokes far more unease than admiration. If you wonder whether the appearance of a strikingly attractive woman on the political scene would create a big stir, and if such a scenario might raise questions about personal authenticity, then perhaps you slept through the whirlwind surrounding Conservative and later Liberal MP Belinda Stronach. From the moment she entered electoral politics in early 2004 through her retirement in the spring of 2007, Stronach was consistently described as the blond, good-looking, well-dressed daughter of auto-parts magnate Frank Stronach. One study, in fact, concluded Stronach's appearance was discussed in a full one-third of the newspaper accounts that mentioned her party leadership bid, while her ties to her father were referred to in one-fifth of those stories.[22]

The media frenzy surrounding Stronach reached its first crescendo in January 2004, when she announced her candidacy for the leadership of the newly merged Conservative party. At that time, her annual income as Magna CEO was estimated at approximately $9 million, and the family's wealth at roughly $625 million.[23] Two years later, writing in *Toronto Life* magazine, journalist Sylvia Fraser recalled the high-voltage atmosphere of Stronach's campaign launch:

> Wearing designer clothes and stilettos, embracing her height as easily as her wealth, the pretty heiress teleprompted her way through a speech about sharing "a bigger economic pie." As reporters looked into the hopeful face, bracketed by perfect blond parentheses, many saw a tall, hot-house poppy in need of trimming: *Who does she think she is?*[24]

As a female politician who pulsed with two colossal assets, wealth and physical beauty, Stronach sent the discomfort meter into high dither. It's no surprise that the unease to which Fraser refers was telescoped into reporters' chosen nickname for this particular leadership campaign. As a play on the phrase "blind ambition," they referred to Stronach's unsuccessful bid against Stephen Harper as "Blond Ambition," and proceeded to dissect her motives for running, her intelligence, and—as discussed in Chapter 4—her two failed marriages.

Stronach later won a House of Commons seat in the June 2004 election that gave Liberal leader Paul Martin a tenuous minority government. Her campaign and victory celebration in the suburban Toronto constituency of

Newmarket-Aurora were presented as follows by *The Globe and Mail*'s Jan Wong:

> She wore Gucci and Prada, styled her blond hair long, and appeared at functions in four-inch stilettos. Last night, she donned a pink poplin suit with white trim by Oscar de la Renta, accessorized with white high heels from Paul Smith Woman…She lives with her two young children in a mansion inside the Magna compound, a Bavarian-style headquarters with a golf course, horse stables, pond, tennis courts, and private gym. Her parents live on the grounds, too, in a separate mansion.[25]

One year later, as the Liberal government's future teetered on a razor-thin edge with an expected budget vote, Stronach secured Paul Martin another eight months in power by switching parties to become a Grit cabinet minister.

Her dramatic, behind-the-scenes decision to leave the Conservatives was not covered, however, as a serious story about political ideas. Even though Stronach carefully explained that she did not share Conservative positions on economic policy, same-sex marriage, or Quebec's future inside Canada, reporters largely ignored this angle. Instead, they seemed obsessed with the romantic side-swipe dimension, namely how Stronach jilted her boyfriend at the time, Tory MP Peter MacKay, in the process of departing one party to join another. Since so much ink and oxygen were devoted to their breakup, and because Stronach's political defection was portrayed as "whoring around" by a top Conservative, I pick up on this highly sexualized part of the story in Chapter 4.

Even in her new incarnation as a Liberal, Stronach remained the target of intensely appearance-focused attention. Media gurus including *Globe and Mail* columnist Margaret Wente reminded readers of father Frank's fortune and daughter Belinda's clothes from "Prada and Gucci."[26] Combining so much ambition, wealth, beauty, and high fashion on the back of one female politician was perhaps too much for such a sparsely-populated country of only 30 million. Ultimately, the woman who stuck out as a "tall poppy" in Sylvia Fraser's account may have reached the same conclusion, as Belinda Stronach announced her decision in 2007 to return to the private sector as Magna's executive vice-chair.

A Voice of One's Own

It's not only age and appearance that female politicians can't seem to calibrate properly. They also, quite literally, can't seem to talk right. "What," you might ask, "in Canada? Aren't we mercifully free of all those British hang-ups about accents and vowels and so on?"

It's true that class percolates less precisely through our speech than it does in the United Kingdom, where Margaret Thatcher reportedly hired a professional coach to ensure she sounded more like the Queen and less like a grocer's daughter from Grantham, the small town where she grew up. What seems to grate in Canada is not so much the socioeconomic underpinnings of speech patterns, but rather the pitch or tone of female politicians' voices. Observers here seem to have a particularly hard time setting aside the assumption that all legislators should express themselves in the honeyed baritones of Brian Mulroney, for example, rather than in a range of other octaves.

Given that women's voices are heard relatively infrequently in Canadian public life, those that sound distinctive tend to be singled out for special, and generally negative, attention. It is not unheard of for men to have voices that sound odd; Preston Manning, for instance, spoke in a way that might have grated on our ears from time to time, but the jarring tones or cadences of Manning and others did not endure as the *sine qua non* of their political reputations. For men in politics, the norm is that we soon begin to disregard their speech format and tune in instead to the content of what they're saying.

For women who sound unusually high-pitched, soft, or otherwise not baritone stentorian, the voice generally becomes the story. The version of the *women plus power equals discomfort* trope that flows from unease about language, therefore, uses particular adjectives—such as "shrill," "strident," "weak," and "squeaky"—to remind us that female tones don't belong in the dark, woody, masculine recesses of Parliament.

The actual content of what's said by women politicians tends to be obscured or even drowned out in this discomfort zone, as listeners reveal their unease with women speakers in the places where men have long ruled. Media accounts, for example, tend to tell us a great deal about style, pitch, and tone—but little about substance. As we saw in the case of judgments about women's ages and physical appearances, female politicians can't seem to get their voices properly modulated either, which means at least some of them are consigned to an incorrect or off-key zone. At one extreme, adopting a pitch that's too deep or a tone that's too authoritative can be castigated as proto-masculine. The other end of the spectrum—as suggested by the discussion of leadership styles in Chapter 2—can be interpreted as overly feminine and tentative, and thus ineffectual.

The latter syndrome came through crystal-clear in commentaries about federal NDP leader Audrey McLaughlin.

Professional experience in social work likely encouraged McLaughlin to develop a soft-spoken, consultative approach to public speaking. Instead of adopting a direct, definitive, and categorical style, McLaughlin seemed to draw her main inspiration from ideas about inclusivity and consensus-seeking in public leadership.

Her own communications advisor, Ian McLeod, later admitted that this "kinder, gentler" oratorical stance was gradually equated "with a failure to set direction," to the point that McLaughlin's style "was perceived as the absence of leadership, the abdication of personal authority."[27] Coming from an NDP insider, McLeod's verdict is hard to dismiss. Indeed, it's difficult to imagine a stronger indictment of niceness and kindness in the realm of public speaking.

Sheila Copps, who worked as a journalist before she ran for public office, represented the polar opposite of McLaughlin in speaking style. Both at the Ontario legislature and in the House of Commons, Copps employed a feisty, conflictual, no-holds-barred approach—whether she was asking questions or heckling across the floor. To the best of my knowledge, no reporter or fellow parliamentarian ever accused Copps of being too quiet, too conciliatory, too wishy-washy, or too much of a white-gloved proper lady.

Yet the very same characteristics that permitted her to escape the criticisms levelled against McLaughlin rebounded in such a way as to label Copps as brash, pushy, and abrasive. Journalists judged Copps to be "strident," in the case of Douglas Fisher writing in *The Toronto Sun*.[28] Susan Delacourt summarized for *Globe and Mail* readers the variety of labels used to describe Copps, including "the famous shrill voice from the opposition benches. Depending on who is talking, she is abrasive, loyal, assertive, down-to-earth, hard-working, noisy, shallow, driven, ambitious, energetic or brazen."[29]

This close association between Copps and a forceful speaking manner meant other dimensions of her political being (including where she stood on the major issues of the day) were conveniently ignored. In retrospect, much of what we're left to recall about her career are capsule stereotypes of how Copps sounded, and how she got under the skin of at least three male colleagues in Parliament—who referred to her using such terms as "baby," "slut," and "bitch."[30] Their allegations are memorable because they show how Copps was far from an anodyne, soft-spoken, and hence well-socialized feminine woman. In fact, the usual depictions of her behaviour made the link from "Copps" to "strident" seem as automatic as that from "Belinda Stronach" to "rich," "blond," and "well-dressed."

Unease over speaking styles affected others besides McLaughlin and Copps, however. Stronach herself was lambasted in the press as rigid and overly scripted, opening up doubts as to whether she was capable of "speaking for herself."[31] In Manitoba, Sharon Carstairs began her career as a schoolteacher and, once she entered provincial politics, built the Liberals from a party with no seats in the legislature to one that attained Official Opposition status. Because Carstairs was an outspoken critic of both the Meech Lake and Charlottetown constitutional accords, she attracted considerable attention in the provincial as well as national media.

The descriptors used in print media stories were rich with gendered meaning, and often sexual innuendo as well. In the words of one newspaper account, Carstairs had a "tightly wound voice and schoolmarmish debating style."[32] Her "red-hot rhetoric" was so "fiery" that it frightened off male voters and created a gender gap for the Manitoba

Liberals.[33] She was "strident, "blunt-speaking," "preachy," "bossy" and, worst of all, projected a "piercing voice."[34] The result of Carstairs having so much "ego drive," reporters told their readers, was that the Manitoba Grits turned into a "one-woman show," and lost ground once the public tired of that one woman.[35]

Journalists also seemed quite uncomfortable with our sole female prime minister, Kim Campbell, since many accounts elided her speaking and leadership styles. Much like Sheila Copps, Campbell was singled out for being too verbally aggressive which was, of course, the flip side of the charge levelled against Audrey McLaughlin. During a 1997 book tour to Australia, Campbell reflected on her experiences with the Ottawa press corps: "I was called arrogant, aggressive and lacking compassion. I don't have a typically female pattern of speech. I'm open and assertive. In men, those traits are perceived as leadership material. In a woman, they are denigrated."[36] Even though she did not reach that conclusion as a neutral, detached assessor, Campbell made a fair enough point. The double standard for confident women in particular meant there was no way to speak, be heard, and at the same time avoid nasty put-downs.

In conclusion, the personal features discomfort zone of Canadian politics has been wide and deep, making it precious difficult for a woman to open her mouth without being found wanting. Self-effacing, soft-spoken players like Audrey McLaughlin have been written off as non-entities, including during crucial election debates when they needed to be noticed. Bold, forceful, outspoken individuals such as Sheila Copps, Sharon Carstairs, and Kim Campbell were accused of being too "in your face."

Unlike in the tale of Goldilocks's visit to the home of the three bears, the story of women politicians in Canada is that they can't seem to get their personal characteristics "just right" no matter how hard they try. Younger women are too young for top jobs, while their veteran counterparts are simply too old. A stunning physical appearance is viewed as unsettling on many levels, while being dowdy doesn't work either. Finding a speaking voice and style that work also constitutes no small challenge.

But the biggest quagmire of all in terms of right and especially wrong involves the sexual discomfort zone for women politicians, discussed next in Chapter 4.

Notes

1. See Linda Trimble, "Who Framed Belinda Stronach? National Newspaper Coverage of the Conservative Party of Canada's 2004 Leadership Race," paper presented at Canadian Political Science Association Meetings, University of Western Ontario, 2005, 5–6.

2. Karen von Hahn, "Hillary Needs to Channel her Inner Beeyatch," *The Globe and Mail* (28 July 2007), L3.

3. See Terry Crowley, *Agnes Macphail and the Politics of Equality* (Toronto: Lorimer, 1990); Doris Pennington, *Agnes Macphail: Reformer* (Toronto: Simon and Pierre, 1989); Margaret Stewart and Doris French, *Ask No Quarter: A Biography of Agnes Macphail* (Toronto: Longmans, Green, 1959).

4. See http://www.statcan.ca/english/research/82-620-MIE/ 2005001/articles/adults/aobesity.htm, consulted 21 September 2007.

5. See www.hc-sc.gc.ca/seniors-aines/pubs/fed_paper/pdfs/ fedpager_e.pdf, consulted 21 September 2007.

6. Sheila Copps, "The Inside Story of a Rookie's Life at Queen's Park," *The Toronto Star* (19 July 1981).

7. Hugh Winsor, "A Dash of Spirit is Added," *The Globe and Mail* (8 December 1981).

8. Lysiane Gagnon, "Sexism Mars the PQ Race," *The Globe and Mail* (24 October 2005), A17.

9. See http://en.wikipedia.org/wiki/Andr%C3%A9_Boisclair, http://en.wikipedia.org/wiki/Parti_Qu%C3%A9b%C3%A9cois_leadership_election%2C_2005, both consulted 21 September 2007.

10. Jeffrey Simpson, "The PQ Has a Funny Way of 'Renewing' Its Leadership," *The Globe and Mail* (15 May 2007), A17.

11. Clinton as quoted in Caroline Heldman, "Cultural Barriers to a Female President in the United States," in Lori Cox Han and Caroline Heldman, eds., *Rethinking Madam President* (Boulder, Colorado: Lynne Reinner, 2007), 29.

12. See http://www.macleans.ca/article.jsp?content=20060313_122948_122948&source=srch, consulted 21 September 2007.

13. One example of these changing winds can be found in comments about Elsie Wayne. Writing in 1983, a freelancer based in Saint John wrote approvingly of her choice of clothes as mayor, concluding Wayne was "always impeccably groomed." See Barbara Carrier, "The Mayor's a Lady Who Aims for Success," *The Globe and Mail* (20 August 1983). Twenty years later, as an Opposition MP, Wayne was mocked by a Liberal cabinet minister for asking about reflective markings on military vehicles while wearing a sequined sweater in the House of Commons. The minister, John McCallum, later apologized. See Daniel Leblanc, "McCallum Regrets Mocking MP's Attire," *The Globe and Mail* (29 January 2003), A4.

14. See http://www.ctv.ca/servlet/ArticleNews/story/CTVNews/20030129/wayne_mccallum_030128?s_name=&no_ads=, consulted 21 September 2007.

15. See Louise Carbert, *Rural Women's Leadership in Atlantic Canada: First Hand Perspectives on Local Public Life and Participation in Electoral Politics* (Toronto: University of Toronto Press, 2006).

16. See *Ottawa Citizen* (3 October 1998), B4.

17. Alexa McDonough as quoted in Elizabeth Goodyear-Grant, "Crafting a Public Image: Women's MPs and the Dynamics of Media Coverage," in Sylvia Bashevkin, ed., *Opening Doors Wider: Women's Political Engagement in Canada* (Vancouver: UBC Press, 2009), 147–66.

18. Nick Hills, "For Broadbent, the West is the Test," *Winnipeg Tribune* (3 July 1975).

19. See Alan Fotheringham, "BC's Mrs. Thatcher Embarrasses Barrett," *The Toronto Star* (14 February 1975); Malcolm Gray, "Has Rosemary Brown's Socialist Image More Style than Substance?" *The Globe and Mail* (20 February 1975); Lisa Hobbs, "Why is Rosemary Running?" *Chatelaine* (July 1975).

20. Lysiane Gagnon, "Sexism Mars the PQ Race," A17.

21. Lysiane Gagnon, "Sexism Mars the PQ Race," A17.

22. The comparable figures for media coverage about personal appearance for Stephen Harper and Tony Clement were one and three percent, respectively. See Trimble, "Who Framed Belinda Stronach?" 11, 16.

23. Sylvia Fraser, "The Belinda Stronach Defence," *Toronto Life* (February 2006), 57.

24. Fraser, "The Belinda Stronach Defence," 57; italics in original.

25. Jan Wong, "Stronach Takes Newmarket Riding by a Hair," *The Globe and Mail*, (29 June 2004), A18.

26. Margaret Wente, "Between Love, Business, and Ambition, Love Generally Winds Up Third," *The Globe and Mail* (18 May 2005), A8.

27. Ian McLeod, *Under Siege: The Federal NDP in the Nineties* (Toronto: Lorimer, 1994), 42, 54, 134.

28. For Douglas Fisher's use of this adjective in *The Toronto Sun* in June 2000, see http://fact.on.ca/news/news0006/tt00060a. htm, consulted 21 September 2007.

29. Susan Delacourt, "Sheila Copps Hoping to Add Liberal leader to Long List of Labels," *The Globe and Mail* (16 January 1990).

30. Copps was referred to as "baby" by Tory minister John Crosbie in 1985, a "slut" by Tory MP Bill Kempling in 1991, and a "bitch" by Reform MP Ian McClelland in 1997.

31. Trimble, "Who Framed Belinda Stronach?" 17.

32. Carstairs had long been "the subject of ridicule for her tightly wound voice and schoolmarmish debating style," according to David Roberts, "Manitoba Caucus Shaken as Carstairs Calls it Quits," *The Globe and Mail* (6 November 1992).

33. This description of Carstairs's rhetoric appeared in Geoffrey York, "Carstairs' Flame is Flickering After Dramatic, Meteoric Rise," *The Globe and Mail* (3 January 1990), A12. "Both private and party polls indicate men have had difficulty voting for the fiery former history teacher," according to Miro Cernetig and David Roberts, "Carstairs Accuses Opponents of Sexist Stance on Hustings," *The Globe and Mail* (10 September 1990).

34. The descriptors "preachy" and "bossy" appeared in York, "Carstairs' flame." Carstairs was termed "blunt-speaking" in Geoffrey York, "Carstairs Considered Resigning over Doubts," *The Globe and Mail* (28 May 1990), A9. She was described as having a "strident style" in George Oake, "Tough Three-Party Race Likely in Manitoba," *The Toronto Star* (11 August 1990). Robert Sheppard described Carstairs as "the Manitoba Liberal leader with the piercing voice and the energy of a buzz saw," "What's Good for the Goose Should be Good for…" *The Globe and Mail* (11 September 1990), A17.

35. Pollster Angus Reid was cited in Miro Cernetig, "Carstairs Support Takes a Beating," *The Globe and Mail* (12 September 1990), A10, as suggesting "Mrs. Carstairs never got beyond the image of the party being a one-woman show."

36. Kim Campbell as quoted in Sally Loane, "Former PM Delights in Male Brain Drain," *The Sydney Morning Herald* (28 November 1997).

4

Vexatious Vixens

Many years ago, very early in my career as a university teacher, I was asked by a major publisher to write a book about women and politics that would be targeted at a popular, general audience. The most exciting dimension of this idea, to the editor who proffered the proposal, was that I would be able to "dish all the dirt" about the sex lives of female politicians. After all, this person told me, "everybody is dying to know" who generates the heat in the sheets of women in public life—or, in some cases, how come there's a chill in their bedding.

Here we are, nearly 30 years later, and the same subject continues to tantalize or, more accurately, titillate. I confess I turned down the offer to write such a book because it struck me as offensive to supplement the already well-tended feeding frenzy that was associated with the private lives of female politicians. My opinion has only grown stronger during the ensuing decades.

In light of this background, permit me to state plainly and directly that the purpose of this chapter is to probe the sources of our compelling interest in the romantic entanglements of women in politics, present evidence that the obsession remains alive and well, and explore the consequences of this ongoing fascination. All the material presented in this chapter is drawn from the public domain—published newspaper accounts, films about politicians, biographies, and memoirs. I have not hidden behind curtains, asked tacky questions, or located a single "deep .

throat" informant. If any dirt gets dished in this rendering, it emerges entirely from my effort to turn the reflecting mirror away from political women, and turn it more closely toward each of us who writes and consumes stories about them.

Let's begin with the perplexing question of why so much ink is spilt and oxygen expended on this subject. Obviously, there must be public interest, because the numbers of eyeballs and ears trained on websites, televisions, newspapers, and radios play a major role in determining what news stories are not just covered but also repeated and revisited.

So, if there is so much interest, where does it come from? We've heard the old saying that power is an aphrodisiac, meaning the reality or, in some cases, appearance of influence and authority can make individuals more sexually attractive than they would otherwise be. In Canada, the ability of a short man with imperfect skin to draw throngs of awestruck women to his every appearance—particularly if he is a middle-aged, intellectually inclined politician rather than a young rock idol—and to provoke something of a public mania as a result, is understandable from this perspective. I refer, of course, to Pierre Trudeau's magnetically charged election campaign in 1968 as the newly anointed leader of the Liberal Party of Canada.

When he served earlier as minister of justice in Lester Pearson's cabinet, and was faced with contentious issues including divorce and abortion, Trudeau famously pronounced that the state has no business in the bedrooms of the nation. Consistent with the spirit of that statement, the nation pretty much left Trudeau alone in the boudoir, whether his entanglements involved the woman who later became his wife, Margaret Sinclair, or other reputed companions including Barbra Streisand, Liona Boyd, and Deborah Coyne.

The intriguing point about Trudeau's experiences is that he was granted a zone of privacy that delineated clear boundaries between his activities as head of government, or as an opposition and later retired politician, on one side, and his personal life on the other. To the extent that Trudeau's various romantic adventures were remarked upon, the commentary was framed either as a kind of high-five triumphalism that our top political executive was sexually active and vibrant, or as a quiet, almost pitiful lament for his having been jilted by Margaret Trudeau.

This chapter reveals a sharp contrast between the respectful treatment accorded Trudeau, and the far more invasive digging and probing that pry well beyond the privacy borders for leading women in Canadian politics. In fact, I would propose that the former justice minister's remark is frequently turned on its head vis-à-vis female politicians, such that *political women's bedrooms become the business of the nation*. In the process, the targets whose private lives are subject to close scrutiny become objectified, sexualized, and typically viewed as loveless spinsters, women of too-easy virtue, or perhaps sexually unsettled individuals.

Rather than standing back at a hushed, dignified distance—as they did for Trudeau—political observers including news reporters tend to get swept up in a vulture-like rush that sees them picking over every sordid detail of a woman's romantic life. Female politicians who appear to be sexually active outside a monogamous heterosexual marriage run into particular difficulties, since they tend to be portrayed as vexatious vixens—demanding, sultry, and not fully on top of their public responsibilities, given these other entanglements. Instead of standing back and either admiring or pitying a public figure—as was done for Trudeau—in the case of targeted political women, we seem willing to revert to adolescent leering. I find this switch to be extremely unsettling, since it suggests that we as average citizens are prepared to allow news organizations to gloss over the difference between their acknowledged legitimate role as sources of political information and commentary, and a far more sinister position as highly selective gatekeepers of public virtue.

How can we explain this differential treatment of the private lives of men versus those of women? Well, if power is an aphrodisiac, and if women are viewed in our culture as the more romantically mysterious and forbidden gender, then it stands to reason (should reason come into the picture at all) that women who are close to or in power would generate higher-magnitude sexual tremors than men. British political scientist Joni Lovenduski points out that since Biblical times, "women have been seen as the lustful sex whose tempting, seducing sexuality was responsible for man's downfall."[1] The unease we unearthed in discussions of their leadership styles, as well as such personal characteristics as age, appearance, and speech, would therefore pale in comparison with the discomfort surrounding the far more loaded realm where sex and power meet.

Tensions over the destabilizing effects of female presence and desire, particularly if mixed up with traces of political clout, hardly ended in the Garden of Eden. They can be discerned in late nineteenth- and early twentieth-century arguments against extending the right to vote. In Canada as elsewhere, suffragists faced the visceral counter-argument that enfranchisement (as well as the related threat of opening up opportunities in other sectors including post-secondary education) would damage women's reproductive capacity, endanger the family, and effectively destroy society as we knew it.

These claims were grounded in a traditional view that females inhabited a separate, pure, and morally superior private sphere, which should remain apart from the corrupting filth of political intrigue. The idea may sound quaintly Victorian, but its echoes continue to resonate in contemporary Canada. We still can discern elements of the split between public and private life, with its rigid gender schemas for political men and apolitical women, in the tendency to find vixen-like characteristics in females who venture beyond conventional boundaries. In fact, the crossing-of-the-lines unease that underpins much of our fascination with the private lives of public women reveals a frisson-charged energy field that yet surrounds them, long after Eve met Adam.

It's also likely that much of this interest follows from women's position as rare birds in the public realm. Given their ongoing low numbers in our city councils and legislatures, female politicians are viewed as unusual creatures and museum-like specimens. Frankly, they stand out as irresistible objects of enduring curiosity, and especially as subjects for ceaseless sexual speculation. From the perspective of political observers, a woman in politics is as remarkable a sight as a bright tropical cockatiel singing on a frosty Canadian park bench. Who wouldn't want to know how it got there, whether it had a mate, and where they nested together?

Taken together, the rarity, dangerous sensuality, and power trappings of women in politics have combined to produce a libidinal fascination that shows no sign of ebbing. I would argue that this dimension of our unease has turned what is for a man the private life of a public figure into what is for each targeted woman a no-holds-barred subject of public discourse.

Well, you might ask, if we're a fair-minded people and were so curious about Belinda Stronach's boyfriends, for example, then why didn't we demand that reporters approach Pierre Trudeau's romantic life in a similarly invasive way? Perhaps this differential treatment is simply a function of the changing communications industry: since the 1980s, the boundaries between personal and public spheres have become less visible and, as a result, less defensible, than they once were. The advent of 24-hour electronic news, for example, creates demand for more footage and commentary, which presses the range of coverage into domains that used to be private. The pattern of constant information saturation only reinforces our appetite for "news" about individuals whose personal visibility has effectively turned them into celebrities.

Counter-arguments of this type are far from convincing. Evidence presented in this chapter shows that media stories about the romantic lives of female politicians in Canada date back nearly a hundred years, to a time well before camcorders and digital photography. The arrival of all-news TV channels and Internet sites may have intensified the search for things to talk about, but they did not independently create a fascination with this subject.

On another plane, let's consider the possibility that journalists held Trudeau in higher esteem, and feared him more, than they have any woman in politics. Or maybe, because most Parliament Hill reporters at the time were heterosexual males, they identified closely with the prime minister's romantic conquests (as well as his jilting at the hands of his wife), and enjoyed the opportunity to bask in the reflected glow of his sexual prowess. This ability to sympathize, empathize, and probably fantasize given their own ups and downs, so to speak, may have led members of the Ottawa press corps to handle Trudeau's personal life with a remarkable degree of discretion.

It is quite possible that the same factors would operate to a far lesser degree in the case of female politicians, and would cause male reporters to cut them minimal slack. Women journalists in this country continue to be few in number and limited in clout in both municipal and parliamentary press galleries.[2] Given the professional challenges they face, female reporters who work the corridors of city halls and legislatures are likely to devote far more attention to securing their own reputations in the eyes of male colleagues, than to nurturing close relations with women in elective office—especially to the point that they would identify with the latter's romantic travails.

The proposition that reporters gaze on politicians in highly gendered ways is entirely believable. Yet, by itself, this can't explain the pulsing herd mentality that rushes to probe the private lives of particular women in Canadian politics—notably Belinda Stronach during recent years, and Kim Campbell before her.

It's important to note that although female politicians as a group are seen as more exotic and sexually charged than their male counterparts, not all of them are probed to the same degree. Not illogically, the individuals who tend to capture the most attention because they are deemed to be the most romantically interesting and most available for open-season-style pursuit have never been married, or are separated or divorced. Given that on average, elected women in Canada are more likely than the men with whom they serve to have these characteristics, it's easy to figure out how reporters find material. Simply stated, few women relative to men populate our public elite, and many among these few tend to evoke considerable libidinous interest. By contrast, political women who more or less "fit" the masculine standard of married with children don't draw nearly the same sexual hype or buzz as those who deviate from that norm.

Assume for a moment that the typical male MP or MLA is a married man whose wife and two children live hundreds of kilometres away in the home constituency. Also imagine that this median man gets lonely from time to time in the capital city where he spends much of his time, and shares the company of another woman. It's fair to imagine that any reporter who contemplates covering this hypothetical politician's extramarital activities is automatically confronted with questions of damage and blame, since what's being speculated on is hardly a victimless offense. A web of tough ethical questions may cut off the story before it ever sees the light of day. They include whether it's the job of journalists to police adulterous liaisons, and if the presumed morality of reporting on immorality is trumped by the embarrassment or humiliation of the various parties.

Given that a considerable number of women politicians who've served in Canada either were never married or were separated or divorced, the constraints on press coverage of them appeared far looser than for men in politics. Speculating on what the single female politician does after hours appears to be a victimless exercise, since there's no need to worry about a hapless spouse holding down the fort back in the hustings. There may of course be small children, or even grown children, but they tend to be entirely absent from the radar screens in this calculus.

My point is that the sexualized treatment of female politicians has numerous and varied sources, but seems to operate fairly selectively. In Canada, it's most pronounced, sustained, and intense for women office-holders who are not in heterosexual marriages.

In terms of consequences, the *women plus power equals discomfort* thesis helps to explain how certain female politicians create palpable unease by shaking up the sexual status quo. The common trope relative to them is similar to the one identified in Chapters 2 and 3: women who deviate from the male model of married with children are unable to get things right in the romance department, and are portrayed as frustrated spinsters, wayward whores, or otherwise sexually troubled individuals. This sexual discomfort zone makes it extremely difficult for women with any family status other than married and heterosexual to hold positions of public leadership. Under the terms of the prevailing tension, then, being a "normal" woman in one's private life is the price of entry to politics. Try something else, the chorus continues, and you'll be placed under the unflattering prism of a high-powered microscope.

Chastity Is a Problem

Given all the Victorian legacies in Canadian architecture and elsewhere, prudery might seem an attractive option for unattached political women. Alas, the experiences of never-married female politicians since World War I reveal major limits to that strategy. In fact, they suggest the reverse, namely that chastity is a problem for single political women.

Why? Primarily because the prevailing interpretation constructs an asexual woman as demonstrating, on one side, personal rigidity, severity, seriousness, and one-dimensional workaholism and, on the other, an alarming absence of fun, humour, and emotional balance. Either way, this framing presents a far from flattering image.

Canada's first woman MP was one of the first to be affected by the chastity-is-a-problem phenomenon. Agnes Macphail, elected in 1921 from the rural seat of South-East Grey, represented the United Farmers of Ontario—a group that was later absorbed into the Cooperative Commonwealth Federation (CCF, precursor to the NDP). She defeated ten men to become her party's candidate, and insisted on contesting the seat even though the South-East Grey constituency association "was besieged by protests" because she, a woman, had been nominated.[3] In Macphail's words, "It took strenuous campaigning for two months just to stop people from saying, 'We can't have a woman.' I won that election in spite of being a woman."[4]

This baptism by fire carried more than a bit of highly conflicted sexual baggage. Although she was portrayed in one *Canadian Forum* caricature as a Girl Guide, which suggested a wealth of modesty and propriety, Macphail was perceived in her local constituency as quite threatening, bold, and lacking an appropriate sense of social boundaries.[5] Macphail described her experiences as those of "a sort of bear in a cage," since she was an unmarried, 31-year-old schoolteacher who flew in the face of the norms of the time by appearing in public without either a hat or gloves.[6] In the words of one biographer, simply being an unattached, politically active, rural woman made her a heretic and harridan: "Scurrilous gossip among opponents in the riding charged that Macphail was 'mannish,' a rival to wives, and a threat to the sanctity of marriage—the normal slander for a single woman venturing into public life."[7]

Since she understood the disjuncture between her gender and the public role of an MP, Macphail reflected at length on the intense glare under which she functioned as a parliamentarian. She described her status as an exotic creature in the following terms: "I couldn't open my mouth to say the simplest thing without it appearing in the papers. I was a curiosity, a freak. And you know the way world treats freaks."[8]

Perhaps because of the sexual threats that had been read into her activities as a federal candidate in South-East Grey, Macphail adopted a very restrained style in Ottawa. She arrived on Parliament Hill wearing a straw hat with veiled brim and a blue serge dress, and carried with her a clutch purse and gloves.[9]

Among the most curious dimensions of the media accounts of Canada's first female MP was the difference between what local reporters and what those based in Ottawa had to say about the threat posed by her single status. Unlike their small-town counterparts, journalists on Parliament Hill believed married women had nothing to fear from Macphail's presence, since she dressed unfashionably and behaved in an argumentative, impatient, and sometimes inscrutable manner.[10] After a speech she delivered in the House of Commons that condemned both the Liberals and Conservatives, a major newspaper headline read as follows: "Progressives have no love for Grits or Tories, dramatically declares Miss Agnes Macphail; Does Agnes know what love is?"[11]

Pre-dating Kim Campbell's remarks roughly 80 years later on the loneliness of being an unmarried woman MP, Macphail gave voice to her own disappointments with life in the nation's capital. One reporter for Toronto's *Evening Telegram* offered a highly charged rebuttal to those observations: "Some people may remind her that it much depends on herself just how long she will be lonely."[12]

We can't know for sure whether that journalist was offering himself as a suitor, but the historical record indicates Macphail turned down a number of marriage proposals, some after her election to Parliament. One is reputed to have come from R.B. Bennett, a leading federal Conservative who went on to serve as prime minister.[13] What remains clear is that her unmarried status was considered a matter worthy of public comment, notably by Quebec premier Louis-Alexandre Taschereau. Offended by Macphail's criticism in 1928 of the lack of a provincial franchise for women in Quebec, Taschereau offered to "serve as her matrimonial agent" so she would not have to spread herself so thin among the 244 MPs who served at the time in Ottawa.[14]

It is difficult to imagine a more sexually loaded remark even in our times, let alone the 1920s. Easier to fathom is the reason why with men like Taschereau in politics, Quebec women waited until 1940 to gain the right to vote in provincial elections, and until 1961 to see the first female member elected to the National Assembly.

Given that she had no spouse or children, reporters trained their sights on the curious question of who looked after Macphail's household. Coming from a modest family background, and with no female colleagues in the Commons, Macphail chose to share an Ottawa apartment with the head of the Senate stenography pool. In the words of Genevieve Lipsett-Skinner, writing for *The Montreal Star* in 1922, "They do their own housework—whoever gets in first puts the kettle on and sets the table."[15]

Macphail was not without witty answers to the tough questions she faced. When heckled by a fellow MP with the proverbial taunt, "Why don't you get yourself a man?" Macphail offered the following rebuttal: "What guarantee have I he wouldn't turn out like you?"[16] Although replies such as this indicate Macphail was no humourless spinster, her acute wit seems to have been lost on the jousting partners who served with her in Parliament. It's worth noting that the reporters and MPs who peppered her with romantic queries expressed no parallel concerns about the lack of a woman in the lives of Mackenzie King or R.B. Bennett.

Canada's first female MP was also fully conscious of the compromises entailed in her decision to pursue a political career. She wrote of "a deep sorrow" at not being "a wife and mother," and wanted future generations of women—

in her own words—to "have it all," meaning fulfilling professional as well as family lives.[17] Macphail recognized that her arrival in Ottawa had been greeted with curiosity mixed with hostility, and realized it emanated from MPs as well as members of the press gallery—including the few women journalists serving at the time on Parliament Hill.[18]

In a commentary published in 1929, Macphail reflected on the origins of this chilly feeling: "I am sure that my plain blue serge suit, my horn-rimmed glasses and my prim attitude frightened a good many."[19] Each of these factors was of course compounded by her sustained engagement with many significant and controversial issues of the day, including war, capital punishment, and prisoners' rights. A busy schedule of speaking, travel, and constituency work left little time for cultivating friendships in the press gallery or developing hobbies outside politics.[20]

The portrayal of single political women as oddities, however, did not end with Agnes Macphail, nor did assumptions that those who shielded their romantic entanglements from media scrutiny led social lives that were deficient, barren, and boring. One has only to recall the coverage of Flora MacDonald's 1976 bid for the federal Progressive Conservative leadership to be reminded of how more recent commentary echoed the views expressed in Macphail's time.

Throughout the 1976 campaign, MacDonald, raised in a large Scottish family in Cape Breton, was described in the media as a red-haired "girl Friday" and a "spinster."[21] Like Macphail, she was presented to the public as a woman who had no existence in her adult life beyond politics. Captions in one magazine account reveal both the strong emphasis on this idea of what she lacked, and the extent to which MacDonald described herself as living in a sterile vacuum that did not resemble the environment in which "normal"

Canadian women operated: "I can barely boil an egg. My job is my life—yes! My constituency is my family."22

MacDonald finished in a very weak sixth place on the first convention ballot in 1976. This outcome wasn't helped by the kind of media coverage she attracted and, indeed, contributed to herself—as reflected in the quotation cited above. MacDonald's social framing limited her chances of success in the leadership race, by portraying her as an overly serious, one-dimensional person who existed far from the "normal" realm of women's routine domestic life. Clearly, most Conservatives, and probably many Canadians, would have had a hard time relating to the candidate thus depicted.

Whether Joe Clark, Brian Mulroney, Pierre Trudeau, or other male partisans of that time could boil an egg or, conversely, repair a leaky washing machine didn't seem to matter. Each of them had a wife, a girlfriend, or children who could dull the edge of wariness about normalcy, because each was arguably a very serious political animal with minimal interests outside that realm. Moreover, unlike either Macphail or MacDonald, each had professional handlers who ensured they avoided any questions about their personal lives that could open up a dangerous, yawning chasm. In the case of both women MPs, that abyss was called "chaste singledom" on Parliament Hill.

Heterosexual Activity Is Also a Problem

Unlike never-married women in politics, those with multiple trips to the altar before they were elected plus active romantic lives while holding public office were unlikely to be accused of lacking zest, exuberance, or a willingness to take risks. Indeed, unlike the stereotypical dour, painfully serious spinster, her counterpart who had visibly loved, dated, and, in the memorable words of Belinda Stronach, refused to "sit at home and knit on Friday nights," was painted with very different strokes.[23] The latter were presented to the citizens of Canada as bold, fickle, superficial, and so distracted by their social lives that they could not be reliably entrusted with other affairs—namely, those of state.

Before she arrived in Ottawa in 1988 as the MP for Vancouver Centre, Kim Campbell had served as a trustee and as chair of the Vancouver school board, as an MLA in the BC legislature, and as a candidate for the leadership of the BC Social Credit party. A graduate of the University of British Columbia's Faculty of Law, she had also studied Soviet politics at the graduate level at the London School of Economics. In 1986, four years after the breakup of her ten-year marriage to UBC mathematics professor Nathan Divinsky, she wedded lawyer Howard Eddy. Journalists who looked into the details of Campbell's marital history noted that both Divinsky and Eddy were politically conservative, highly intelligent, musically talented, and considerably older than Campbell. Each had children from a previous marriage, and reporters spent some time researching just how good a stepmom Campbell was to their offspring.[24]

Soon after her arrival, Campbell became a highly visible politician on Parliament Hill. In 1990, Brian Mulroney appointed her as Canada's first female minister of justice and, three years later, as the first woman to hold the national defence portfolio. During her time in cabinet, Campbell grappled with a number of issues that were not only controversial, but also intensely gendered. They included abortion, the admissibility of a woman's sexual history in rape trials, and gun control in the wake of the killing in 1989 of 14 young women at Montreal's École

Polytechnique. The nature of the bills she introduced meant Campbell remained a highly visible cabinet minister. For the most part, feminist critics argued she'd not gone far enough in defending women's interests, while opponents on the political right portrayed her as a committed fellow traveller with those same feminists.[25]

It was more the smouldering, sultry side of Campbell that caught on like wildfire in 1992 and following. That year marked the publication of one photograph and the delivery of one speech that set tongues wagging across the country and beyond. The photo, taken by Barbara Woodley for a book about famous Canadian women, showed a slightly bemused, bare-shouldered Campbell standing in front of billowy sheer curtains, holding out her silk Queen's Counsel robes on a wooden hanger. The day after an exhibition of Woodley's portraits opened at the National Arts Centre, Campbell's photo appeared on the front page of the *Ottawa Citizen*.

Once published, the shot set off a storm of commentary. NDP MP Lynn Hunter "called the pose inappropriate and labelled Campbell the 'Madonna of Canadian politics.'"[26] At the opposite end of the spectrum, right-wing columnist Allan Fotheringham saw the image as a welcome jolt to the body politic: "Anytime you have a blonde with bare shoulders in March in the middle of a recession, the political libido has to bounce."[27] Peter C. Newman, the grand pooh-bah of Canadian journalism, pronounced her "perky, smart, sexy."[28] A leading Quebec commentator, Michel Vastel, pounced on the distinct societies dimension of the story; in his words, "the only question which interested the English media was whether she was in the nude behind the robe… nobody asks what she has in her head."[29]

Like Agnes Macphail, however, Kim Campbell did not exactly revel in this capital fishbowl. After her second husband moved out of their Ottawa home in early 1991, rumours swirled about Campbell's involvement with John Tait, who served at the time as her deputy minister in the Department of Justice. When invited in late 1992 to speak before a group of mostly female journalists about life as a woman in politics, Campbell took the opportunity to question her own media framing, and especially the use of the phrase "crushingly ambitious" in an earlier *Toronto Star* column by Rosemary Speirs. In Campbell's words,

> What is "crushingly ambitious?" I find it extra-ordinary, because in the course of my life in Ottawa my marriage has ended and I'm very far from home. I find life here often unspeakably lonely and very difficult…What is it about a woman's success or a woman's aspirations that triggers that term? It reminds me of the old definitions we used to circulate at law school about how a man is forceful, a woman is pushy. A man stands his ground, a woman is a complaining bitch… We cannot encourage women to participate and then punish them for their successes, for the effrontery of aspiring to do more.[30]

By taking on the national affairs columnist for Canada's largest circulation daily, Campbell displayed a feisty, risk-taking approach to life in the public spotlight.

Her victory six months later in the Progressive Conservative leadership race, which brought with it the keys to 24 Sussex Drive, was attributable in no small part to the headline-grabbing, high-wire act that began with Woodley's photo. The problem was that this same boldly adventurous approach to public life, with its rejection of restraint, diffidence, and self-effacing modesty, was turned on its head in both the leadership and subsequent election races.

Supporters of Jean Charest, Campbell's main opponent in the party leadership contest, insisted he was a far better choice to head the party. As a "stable" family man with a wife and children, Charest was not tainted by the volatile "unpredictability" and "brittleness" that characterized Campbell.[31] Moreover, even though she had years of post-secondary education and more experience in cabinet than either Trudeau or Mulroney possessed before becoming prime minister, Campbell was chided for running a glitzy, superficial campaign dominated by "Hollywood glamour."[32]

This rhetoric seeped into the subsequent general election campaign, as pro-Charest jabs against Campbell became fodder for critics outside the party. The new Conservative leader was portrayed as a two-time divorcée with an unsettled social life, an unabashed readiness to speak her mind, and a resulting possible unsuitability for top public office. Allegations that Campbell could not remain focused on what mattered continued through the 1993 campaign, as reporters buzzed with stories of the time she spent with boyfriend Gregory Lekhtman rather than studying briefing binders or attending political events.[33]

Campbell chafed at what she described in a December 1993 *Maclean's* interview as "this prurient interest in my private life." The former prime minister stated that she did not know the reason for such intense media interest while she was in public life, and suggested that "one of the compensations of not being prime minister is to have both the time and privacy to pursue it [a social life]. It's just such an invasion of my privacy to be talking about that."[34] The stories continued long after Campbell retired from federal politics; for example, in 2000, a feature in *The Globe and Mail* described Hershey Felder, now her husband of twelve years, as one of the "hard-bodied toy boys" favoured by older women.[35]

All told, Campbell successfully avoided the main charges levelled against Macphail and MacDonald. She was clearly not a ponderous, all-work-no-play, lifetime single. The downside was that she developed an equally damaging image that presented her as too passionate, too shallow and, let's be honest, too sexually hot for such a cold country.

The Power of Money Is Limited

What might have happened had Agnes Macphail, Flora MacDonald, or Kim Campbell possessed unlimited resources to dodge the various swipes that came at them? What if Macphail, for example, had owned more than a couple of dresses? Or if MacDonald and Campbell had commanded armies of spin doctors and handlers to manage the media hoards, and thus ensured they avoided self-inflicted image injuries?

For the sake of laboratory-like experimentation, we in Canada are fortunate to have had an opportunity to test the effect of money. Belinda Stronach's arrival on the federal political scene in January 2004, when she announced her candidacy for the leadership of the merged Alliance and Progressive Conservative parties, offered a chance to explore the media portrayal of an extremely affluent single woman politician; someone who for practical purposes had no ceiling on her clothing, staff, housing, entertainment, or other personal budgets. As a twice-married divorcée, like Campbell, would Stronach manage to more expertly navigate the swirling currents of life by the Rideau Canal?

As of this writing, the answer is assuredly "no." Stronach failed in her bid for the top Tory party post, switched to the Liberals in 2005 under a storm of highly sexualized commentary, and then two years later announced her retirement from federal politics, in April 2007 at the age of 40. Clearly, Stronach might return to elective office at some future date, steeled by her earlier experiences and perhaps better able to defend her private sector credentials—including her independent contributions to Magna International, the firm established by her father.

In the meantime, the shadow under which Stronach operated as an unmarried but romantically active MP did not appear any easier to escape than the one examined in Chapter 3, which loomed over her appearance (too many expensive designer outfits) and social class (not self-made, ergo an inauthentic aristocrat). In fact, the financial resources that Belinda Stronach brought to her political career not only failed to convert into the power to tone down a highly sexualized image, but also effectively made the potion more incendiary. Instead of neutralizing the mixture of her physical allure, romantic availability, and proximity to centres of influence, Stronach's wealth created an even more potent brew.

How can I make such a claim? First, multiple bulging folders in my file drawers, full of press clippings about Stronach, offer a measure of the ink spilt on her. Let's bear in mind that she was actively engaged in party leadership and electoral politics for a total of three years and a few months—meaning Stronach drew, for a Canadian politician, remarkable quantities of print media attention during a fairly short period. This volume of coverage is even more notable when you consider that for most of her time in the eye of the media hurricane, Stronach was not at the apex of the political pyramid; that is, not serving as a party leader, deputy party leader, or top-ranking cabinet minister.

Second, it's the content of much of the material that reveals the strength of the mixture of looks, availability, politics, and money. Unlike news accounts of Kim

Campbell, which generally dissected and judged her personal life in fairly subtle ways, much of the coverage of Belinda Stronach was flat-out invasive. This may mirror an increasingly celebrity-oriented approach to Canadian political news that unfolded between 1993 and 2004, effectively turning parties and legislatures into entertainment venues. During this time, it seemed political actors didn't so much debate significant matters of public import, but rather engaged in high drama, vapid farces, and romantic tragedies that were then served up for public titillation. To wit, during their leadership race, newspaper stories mentioned Stronach's marital status four times as often as they did that of fellow contender Stephen Harper.[36]

When she announced her candidacy for the merged Conservative party leadership in 2004, Stronach was 37 years old, with one year of university education and two unsuccessful marriages behind her. She and her first husband, Magna executive Donald Walker, shared custody of their two children, who were also said to be close with Stronach's second partner, Norwegian speed-skating champion Johann Olav Koss.[37] The two marriages lasted approximately five years and two years, respectively.

What else had Stronach done with her life by the age of 37? Well, as noted in Chapter 3, much of her world had revolved around her father's various entrepreneurial and philanthropic activities. She'd served on the Magna corporate board, as a human resources vice-president and as a judge for the Magna Scholarship prizes. Branching out beyond the formal boundaries of the firm, Stronach had invested in the fashion business and was contemplating a role in John F. Kennedy Jr's magazine enterprise the same week that his plane crashed in 1999.[38]

As someone who circulated in the global social stratosphere, Stronach came into contact with one of the world's most renowned inhabitants of the nexus of sex and power, former US president Bill Clinton. From the time they first met in 2001, Stronach and Clinton were linked romantically by tabloid commentators, who tagged her with the nickname "Bubba's babe."[39] Whether their liaison was entirely political, charitable, and otherwise platonic—as both insisted—was hardly relevant. The point is that Stronach was widely photographed at Clinton's side, and became known to Canadians as an attractive, fun-loving, globe-trotting, and well-connected blond heiress.

This was all fine and good as long as she remained in the shielded realm of private business. What took the lid off the cauldron and sent plumes of steam in all directions was Stronach's decision to seek public office, first as a party leader and then as the MP for Newmarket-Aurora. The question of how she spent her evenings, weekends, and spare time generally sent reporters in staid Ottawa into a veritable research frenzy. Who would the rich party gal hook up with next?

After she lost to Stephen Harper in the 2004 leadership race, Stronach won the Newmarket-Aurora seat for the Conservatives in the 2004 election. Her caucus activities did not attract much media attention until she arrived at the March 2005 party convention holding hands with fellow Conservative MP Peter MacKay. MacKay, then deputy party leader, held the same Nova Scotia constituency that his father Elmer had temporarily vacated in 1983, permitting Brian Mulroney to win a seat in the Commons as Opposition leader. Peter MacKay was young, handsome, and dynamic, and like Stronach, a well-connected, reasonably moderate partisan who did not want to see the Conservatives lurch into the dark reaches of the far right.

Their appearance as a smiling political couple set jaws shuddering. Readers of the national newspaper of record were treated to an extensive description of the jacket, trousers, shoes, and makeup Stronach wore at the Tory convention.[40] It seemed that Conservative leader Stephen Harper was far from pleased at being upstaged by the caucus duo, to the point that he reportedly kicked over a bunch of empty chairs in full view of the press.[41] Subsequent accounts indicated Harper had no patience with Stronach's support that spring for same-sex marriage, or her efforts to slow down the locomotive for defeating the budget of the minority Liberal government, which would result in a quick election call.

Yet almost no one was prepared for the consequences of this tension between Stronach and Harper. On the morning of 17 May 2005, Stronach arrived at the National Press Building in Ottawa on the arm of Liberal prime minister Paul Martin, and announced she was switching parties to become Canada's minister of human resources. In the mass of stories that followed this meteoric event, very limited attention was paid to the substantive policy reasons why Stronach was defecting. Instead, the major feeding frenzy surrounded her desertion of both her beau of ten months, Peter MacKay, and her party. Reams of stories portrayed MacKay as the sad, jilted suitor, hugging his trusty dog back home in Nova Scotia to get away from the glare of the cameras in Ottawa. Others reported the heated rants of Conservative elites, one of whom condemned Stronach's decision as "whoring herself out to the Liberals."[42]

Once the tempest over her defection had passed, Stronach went back to being among the most eligible women in the country. Press accounts continued to speculate over the nature of her ties to Bill Clinton. She was named in divorce papers in the fall of 2006 as the cause of former Toronto Maple Leafs enforcer Tie Domi's marital breakup. And so the saga continued until, just before her 41st birthday, Stronach announced she was quitting public life to return to Magna. As she told CTV's Mike Duffy in the midst of the Domi divorce proceedings, women in Canadian politics face "a double standard" that involves more scrutiny of their private lives than men receive. In Stronach's words, "When I decided to enter public life, I didn't realize how public it would be."[43]

Sexual Diversity Poses Problems

To this point, we've only considered the frisson that's surrounded single, presumably heterosexual women politicians. What about the treatment of other sexual orientations, especially lesbianism, in public office?

Given the scarcity of empirical materials in this area, it's difficult to respond to this question beyond observing that homosexuality among female politicians (whether perceived or real) would appear to send the discomfort meter into spasms. Research on New Zealand party leader and prime minister Helen Clark shows that as a childless career politician married to a man, she faced what one account termed an ongoing "whispering campaign" that included claims she had won the top Labour post thanks to a "lesbian conspiracy" in the party. At least one public allegation was levelled by an audience member at a leaders' debate that she was a "no-kids lesbo."[44] Yet Clark won successive elections as Labour leader despite having regularly to "fend off claims that she is lesbian and that her marriage is a sham."[45]

Allison Brewer, the first and thus far only publicly identified lesbian to hold a top party post in Canada, briefly led the New Brunswick NDP. Two scholars based in that province, Joanna Everitt and Michael Camp, undertook a close study of the coverage in New Brunswick dailies of Brewer's announcement of her candidacy in May 2005, through the subsequent party leadership campaign and provincial election, ending with her resignation as party leader in November 2006.

Everitt and Camp concluded that unease with Brewer's sexuality was so severe that it was referred to in direct as well as coded language. Their quantitative analysis of newspaper accounts showed Brewer was most frequently presented in headlines and press stories as a lesbian, a human rights and disability rights activist, and an abortion rights activist. Taken together, these three descriptions accounted for roughly 80 percent of the media references to Brewer during her short career as leadership candidate and party leader. Everitt and Camp demonstrate that Brewer's interest in other issues including unemployment, the environment, and social policy were fully overlooked in the rush by print reporters to focus on her sexuality.

Little direct probing of the details of Brewer's personal life appeared in the mainstream New Brunswick media, aside from a series of references to her role as a single parent with a disabled child. This finding might appear at first glance to be a sign that journalists were willing to grant Brewer a fairly wide zone of privacy. Yet the use of headlines such as "NDP chooses lesbian activist as new leader; Alison Brewer wins easily on the first ballot" shows reporters did not need to probe specific romantic entanglements to make the point about this leader's sexuality.[46] In fact, by frequently reminding readers that she belonged to a sexual minority group, and that she was also a veteran social movement campaigner, their stories presented Brewer as an actor from outside the usual parameters of New Brunswick politics. As Everitt and Campbell conclude, "It would seem declared lesbians are by definition 'activists'—perhaps with the corollary proposition that their very existence in full view of the public remains a radical political statement."[47]

It is possible to maintain, of course, that Brewer was fortunate to avoid the kind of speculative extravaganza that surrounded accounts of the personal lives of Campbell or Stronach at the federal level. Perhaps Brewer, as a pioneer figure, was spared this treatment in much the same way as Macphail and MacDonald escaped deep microscopic evaluation in their careers. Either way, we know Brewer quit the New Brunswick political scene only months after her party was badly defeated in the 2006 provincial elections. The setback suffered by the NDP that year confirmed the party's already marginal status and risked associating a leader who was not just a woman but also a lesbian with bad results at the polls.

Conclusions

So what? Why should the sexualization of women politicians matter to us as citizens? Does it make any difference whether we're treated to detailed dissections of the lives of elected women who operate outside the standard confines of heterosexual marriage?

At one very fundamental level, it is important, and that's at the stage of political recruitment. Why would a woman who values her own privacy and that of those close to her willingly subject herself to this experience? If even Belinda Stronach with deep protective reserves of cash and staff could not circumvent the problem, then what mere mortal on the social class scale could hope to survive this fishbowl experience? Statistics Canada reported in 2006 that for the first time since national census data were gathered in 1871, a majority of adult Canadians were unmarried.[48] Therefore, more than half of the women in the country are likely to have a spotlight trained on them should they enter public life. We risk wasting this far from negligible human resource—unless we alter the terms under which female politicians experience politics.

Second, the sexual frisson we've explored detracts directly from the substantive heft or weight of political women. Looking back at the year 1984, we can recall Liberal leader John Turner patting the derrière of party president Iona Campagnolo, who patted him right back. Commentators at the time set out the core question pretty directly: Can a stylish, attractive, and seemingly sexually available woman like Campagnolo be a serious public leader? Turner's critics answered that query with a resounding yes, and he had to humbly beg their pardon for his behaviour.

More than 20 years later, the same question still hangs in the ether. And unless we as citizens start to demand more balanced, fair, and policy-focused coverage of women in public life—particularly for unmarried female politicians—the assumption is going to remain that the two roles are fundamentally incompatible.

In Chapter 6, I suggest some concrete ways we can try to challenge the troublesome framing of women in politics, not only by reporters but also by men in politics and by female politicians themselves. Before turning to those ideas, however, it is crucial to set out some of the broader parameters within which we will need to implement reform.

Notes

1. Joni Lovenduski, *Feminizing Politics* (Cambridge: Polity, 2005), 33.

2. In the words of Pippa Norris, "newsrooms continue to be disproportionately white, male, and middle class." See Pippa Norris, "Introduction: Women, Media, and Politics," in Norris, ed., *Women, Media, and Politics* (New York: Oxford University Press, 1997), 10. Canadian data on women's continued underrepresentation in newsrooms and editorial positions can be found in Gertrude J. Robinson and Armande Saint-Jean, "From Flora to Kim: Thirty Years of Representation of Canadian Women Politicians," in Helen Holmes and David Taras, eds., *Seeing Ourselves: Media, Power and Policy in Canada* 2nd ed. (Toronto: Harcourt, Brace, 1996), 29, 32.

3. Margaret Stewart and Doris French, *Ask No Quarter* (Toronto: Longmans, Green, 1959), 56.

4. Agnes Macphail, "Men Want to Hog Everything," *Maclean's* (15 September 1949), 72.

5. On the Girl Guide portrayal, see Terry Crowley, *Agnes Macphail and the Politics of Equality* (Toronto: Lorimer, 1990), 42.

6. Macphail as quoted in Crowley, *Agnes Macphail*, 48.

7. See Crowley, *Agnes Macphail*, 48–49

8. Macphail, "Men Want to Hog Everything," 72.

9. See Doris Pennington, *Agnes Macphail: Reformer* (Toronto: Simon and Pierre, 1989), 43.

10. See Crowley, *Agnes Macphail*, 57–59.

11. See Pennington, *Agnes Macphail: Reformer*, 114.

12. March 1922 newspaper reports as quoted in Crowley, *Agnes Macphail*, 59.

13. See Pennington, *Agnes Macphail: Reformer*, 113.

14. Taschereau as quoted in Pennington, *Agnes Macphail: Reformer*, 114; Crowley, *Agnes Macphail*, 89.

15. Lipsett-Skinner as quoted in Pennington, *Agnes Macphail: Reformer*, 44.

16. Macphail as quoted in Pennington, *Agnes Macphail: Reformer*, 114.

17. Macphail as quoted in Pennington, *Agnes Macphail: Reformer*, 113, 114.

18. See Pennington, *Agnes Macphail: Reformer*, 42–43.

19. Macphail as quoted in Pennington, *Agnes Macphail: Reformer*, 43.

20. See Pennington, *Agnes Macphail: Reformer*, 43, 44.

21. MacDonald's status as a "girl" was emphasized in Tom Hazlitt, "Girl's Fight for an 'Independent' Canada," *The Toronto Star* (7 May 1971). For references to her as a "spinster," see Frank Jones, "Flora MacDonald is Finding Her Kind of People," *The Toronto Star* (1 March 1975); and Heather Robertson, "Delivering Politics Back to the People," *The Canadian Magazine* (3 May 1975).

22. Robertson, "Delivering Politics."

23. Stronach as quoted in Don Martin, *Belinda: The Political and Private Life of Belinda Stronach* (Toronto: Key Porter, 2006), 36. This quotation appeared in the title of a feature story by Michael Valpy, "Belinda: I Don't Sit at Home and Knit on Friday Nights," *The Globe and Mail* (30 September 2006), F9.

24. See Robert Fife, *Kim Campbell: The Making of a Politician* (Toronto: HarperCollins, 1993), 42, 146–147. On Campbell's marital background, see also Frank Davey, *Reading "Kim" Right* (Vancouver: Talonbooks, 1993); Murray Dobbin, *The Politics of Kim Campbell: From School Trustee to Prime Minister* (Toronto: Lorimer, 1993).

25. See Dobbin, *The Politics of Kim Campbell*, chaps. 3, 4.

26. Hunter as quoted in Fife, *Kim Campbell*, 156.

27. Fotheringham as quoted in Davey, *Reading "Kim" Right*, 140.

28. Newman as quoted in Davey, *Reading "Kim" Right*, 165.

29. Vastel as quoted in Robinson and Saint-Jean, "From Flora to Kim," 33.

30. Campbell as quoted in Fife, *Kim Campbell*, 149–150.

31. Former prime minister Joe Clark endorsed Charest in the belief he would be "calm," while Clark's wife Maureen McTeer supported Charest as a "stable" candidate. Those who maintained Charest was preferable because he had a family included Conservative MP Terry Clifford and Southam columnist Rory Leishman. See Davey, *Reading "Kim" Right*, 132–133. According to Dobbin, one poll of party delegates showed 45 percent of them viewed Campbell's major

weakness as an "arrogant/unstable personality," *The Politics of Kim Campbell*, 145. The description of Campbell as unpredictable and brittle, in contrast to Charest's "likeable demeanor," appeared in an unsigned editorial in *The Globe and Mail* on 9 June 1993. See Davey, *Reading "Kim" Right*, 157; as well as Fife, *Kim Campbell*, 197 ff.

32. *The Globe and Mail* (9 June 1993) as quoted in Davey, *Reading "Kim" Right*, 158.

33. Campbell recalled this coverage in her memoir. See Kim Campbell, *Time and Chance: The Political Memoirs of Canada's First Woman Prime Minister* (Toronto: Doubleday, 1996), 373.

34. Campbell as quoted in Warren Carragata, "A Very Strong Person," *Maclean's* (6 December 1993), 19.

35. Alexandra Gill, "Dating Young: How Kim Campbell Got Her Groove Back," *The Globe and Mail* (22 July 2000), R1, R6.

36. Linda Trimble, "Who Framed Belinda Stronach? National Newspaper Coverage of the Conservative Party of Canada's 2004 Leadership Race," paper presented at Canadian Political Science Association Meetings, University of Western Ontario, 2005, 13.

37. See Martin, *Belinda*, 105.

38. See Martin, *Belinda*, 97.

39. See Martin, *Belinda*, 104.

40. Jane Taber, "Stronach-MacKay Duo Making Splash at Convention," *The Globe and Mail* (18 March 2005), A4.

41. See Martin, *Belinda*, 171.

42. Alberta Conservative MLA Tony Abbott, as quoted in Sylvia Fraser, "The Belinda Stronach Defence," *Toronto Life* (February 2006), 56.

43. Stronach as quoted in Oliver Moore, "Deal Reached in Domi Divorce Battle," *The Globe and Mail* (27 September 2006), A3.

44. Linda Trimble, Natasja Treiberg, and Gabrielle Mason, "Beating (Up) the Boys: Newspaper Coverage of Helen Clark in New Zealand Elections, 1996–2005," paper presented at Canadian Political Science Association meetings, University of British Columbia, 2008, 12.

45. Jennifer Curtin, "Reconciling Gender, Feminism and Party Identity: Women and Political Leadership in New Zealand

and Australia," paper presented at Canadian Political Science Association meetings, University of British Columbia, 2008, 18.

46. This headline appeared in the *Saint John Telegraph Journal* on 26 September 2005. See Everitt and Camp, "One is Not Like the Others: Allison Brewer's Leadership of the New Brunswick NDP," in Sylvia Bashevkin, ed., *Opening Doors Wider: Women's Political Engagement in Canada* (Vancouver: UBC Press, 2009), 127–44.

47. Everitt and Camp, "One is Not Like the Others."

48. See http://www.cbc.ca/canada/story/2007/09/12/census-families. html?ref=rss, consulted 25 September 2007.

5

Pincer Movements

If the unease surrounding women in public life is indeed as serious and consequential as I've argued thus far, then why hasn't more been done about it? First, there's no simple solution that will alter the *women plus power equals discomfort* equation. Chapter 6 suggests a number of concrete steps we can take to make politics more open and attractive to more citizens, but none of them will prove quick or easy to achieve. That's because of a second phenomenon that involves the prevailing climate of ideas in Canada about democracy and representation. The current political environment on both the right and left creates a pincer movement that constrains public involvement—especially for women—and permits all the patterns detailed thus far to continue.

So, you ask, what's wrong with our current circumstances? Quite simply, formal politics has been devalued to the point that few talented people, men or women, bother to vote, let alone join a political party, contest public office, or serve as an elected official. From the political right, conservatives insist that the private sector is where the action is. Conversely, they view the state as either largely moribund, except as a tool for advancing and, in hard times, rescuing business interests, or else as a troublesome, interfering (in the affairs of the market) problem child that needs to be tightly controlled.

The economic libertarian ideas behind what's called "neo-conservatism" or sometimes "neo-liberalism" have been ascendant in many Anglo-American political systems, including Canada's, for about three decades. Since Margaret Thatcher became Tory party leader in Britain during the mid-1970s, we've heard again and again that individuals are responsible for themselves, and that, in her inimitable words, "There is no such thing as society. There are individual men and women and there are families."[1]

These same values that elevated the market, denigrated the state, and glorified self-seeking libertarianism, also pushed traditional notions of citizen engagement toward the margins of public life. Across the developed world in the late 1970s and following, a pronounced shift to the right in the discourse of political elites elevated individualist notions of order, duty, responsibility, and respect, while weakening the primacy of core collectivist norms and principles, including participation, representation, equality, and social justice.

The importation of economic thinking to the realm of politics celebrated the power of independent individuals to make choices in a competitive marketplace. It led many people to see themselves as clients, taxpayers, or customers of a state that was properly subservient to business interests. Thatcher's normative universe was governed by a fundamental emphasis on personal self-sufficiency, even though the country she led and those that had spun off from it (including Canada) were already highly individualistic relative to other democratic systems, including those in continental Europe. Thatcher questioned what collective action had ever done for her, and viewed the idea of people working together—especially to challenge the neo-conservative order—as unnecessary, misguided, undisciplined, and part of an unruly attempt to "get away with mayhem."[2]

From the perspective of the future of democracy, it is unfortunate that many of neo-conservatism's harshest critics on the left fundamentally agreed with their opponents on one crucial point: namely, that electoral and legislative politics no longer mattered. Organized protest against neo-liberalism did bubble up all over the place, from anti-globalization demonstrations beginning in Seattle in 1999 to anti-poverty marches in Quebec, anti-logging protests in Ontario and British Columbia, and so on. Yet what's notable about these various activities is that each occurred outside parliaments, city council chambers, and other mainstream deliberative bodies.

As critics spilled into city streets and beyond, they targeted supranational institutions like the World Bank and the International Monetary Fund as major drivers of the core normative directions of our times. This approach meant that nation-state governments and their core executive and legislative institutions were not only largely ignored, but also seemingly irrelevant. Moreover, when governments did respond to anti-globalization demonstrations, they often operated in such a way as to criminalize political opposition, notably by arresting protesters and even ordering police to attack them. This approach differed from what typically occurred during earlier postwar decades, when demonstrators in Canada and elsewhere were more likely to be respected or at least tolerated for expressing divergent points of view.

The implications of these developments remain unsettling on many levels. For one thing, they deepened an existing dichotomy between the status quo, business-as-usual world of formal politics and the adventurous domain of extraparliamentary activity. Against this background, it's easy to see why rates of participation in elections and party organizations generally declined across much of North America and Western Europe. Voter turnout in Canada consistently fell below 70 percent in federal elections following 1993, after remaining above that level for most of the post–World War II period.[3] Given that turnout was particularly low among younger voters, it seems that citizens who came of age in the Thatcher years and following duly absorbed the powerful message that states don't count.

Unfortunately, this perspective carried considerable weight at both the left and right ends of the ideological spectrum. Progressive young people who did want to engage politically were encouraged by the heroes of the extraparliamentary left, including the überpopular Canadian writer and activist Naomi Klein, to direct their energies away from formal institutions, especially those of the conventional nation-state.[4] The proper targets of protest were identified as global corporations, international economic organizations, and capitalist development in general. Critics on the left celebrated and elevated the status of local issue-based groups and global protest coalitions, to the point that they seemed far more exciting and effective than political parties or, heaven forbid, city councils or legislatures.

Formal state institutions were thus directly eclipsed by developments on both the right and the left. In Canada, this two-pronged, pincer-like devaluation of mainstream public engagement unfolded in quiet but unmistakable steps. The ideational push from the right was less sharply defined, and less visibly charged with religious content, than parallel trends in the United States. The retreat by the extraparliamentary left, such that it essentially evacuated the mainstream terrain by ignoring elections, legislatures, and cabinets, also occurred quietly and gradually. Yet as a compound effect of patterns on both the right and left, a massive silence now surrounds the core values of democratic engagement. In fact, we barely seem to care whether Canadians of any background affirm the importance of citizen participation by engaging in the life of the polity.

This reality stands before us in relatively muted and quite civil (how Canadian!) terms. This country has not faced the ominous threat of a military takeover, nor have opposition politicians been thrown in jail for criticizing the party in power. But the muffled rumblings that threaten the fabric of our democracy from the right, alongside their echoes on the left, are no less daunting because they seem so harmless. In fact, it's the silent, stealthy, pincer-like nature of the process that has made the challenge to parliamentary democracy especially hard to pin down and resist.

This chapter shows how the devaluing of democratic cornerstones like institutional participation and representation, and their eclipsing by an iconic virtue drawn from the economic marketplace—namely, individual choice—holds particular implications for women. Economic conservatives ensured business interests were securely ensconced on their own heavenly plane in the polity. At the same time, they questioned the legitimacy of less privileged claimants for public voice—whether these shared gender (in the case of feminist groups), class (which was critical for trade unions), or other identities. As Susan Faludi famously showed in 1991 with respect to women in the United States, this process constituted an organized backlash against collective interests other than business groups, which weakened older notions that noncorporate entities needed to be represented in politics.[5] To be blunt, if a group no longer exists as a legitimate public entity, then the idea of ensuring or enhancing its political representation also disappears off the radar screens.

Social conservatives embellished this view with their own dangerous patina drawn from the realm of fundamentalist and evangelical religion. The perspectives of the Christian right, which attracted support from traditionalist sects outside Christianity, explicitly defined women as creatures of the home, the family, and the private sphere generally. According to this view, females were not meant to be the same properly self-seeking individualists as males. Instead, they were personal supports for the rational male actor known as "economic man," at his side to encourage him, comfort him, and bear and raise his children. This perspective framed women as dependent, politically impaired creatures, unlike men who were free, unfettered, and autonomous individuals.[6]

The threat posed generally to institutional participation by the rise of neo-conservatism, and the shadow that loomed above women in particular because of the views of the social right, crept up quietly in Canada. The challenge posed by both trends was hardly noticed, I suggest, because critics on the left largely echoed the right's dismal view of formal politics. During the 1980s and following, anti-globalization campaigners pretty much withdrew from mainstream political engagement. Not incidentally, this withdrawal was imitated by the country's leading feminist umbrella group, which spent years embroiled in nasty internecine conflicts that did little to challenge the fundamentally conservative trajectory of the times.

The threat posed by neo-liberalism's trajectory, combined with a retreat from formal politics by many on the left and the ongoing battles among women's movement insiders, neatly obscured the sorts of problems I've detailed in earlier chapters of this book. Essentially, the issue of women's participation in mainstream political institutions largely vanished from public view.

Movement Problems

How did we in Canada reach a point where concerns about citizen participation and group representation have so little traction? This section shows how the problem of women's involvement went missing inside a peak national organization that was ostensibly established to widen public engagement.

The 1970 release of the *Report of the Royal Commission on the Status of Women* marked the start of a concerted, Canada-wide effort to extend women's political involvement beyond the rights to vote and hold public office. Two years later, the National Action Committee on the Status of Women (NAC) was founded as an umbrella organization to press for the implementation of the report's 167 recommendations. These included specific proposals to ensure the election of more women to deliberative bodies across the country.

NAC's early presidents vigorously pursued the goal of enhanced political representation. Representing the full array of major parliamentary parties, and from established status of women and trade union groups, women including Laura Sabia, Lorna Marsden, and Lynn McDonald believed the internal practices of party organizations deserved careful scrutiny. Did party recruiters treat women strictly as volunteers who made coffee and sandwiches for male candidates? How did party headquarters react to efforts by women to secure nominations in winnable seats?

NAC's first-generation leaders also pressed the parties to defend their platforms to female voters, who constituted more than half the citizens of Canada and of the world. It probably reached its peak of public visibility and credibility in 1984 by sponsoring a televised leaders' debate during the federal election campaign. This debate, centred on matters of particular concern to Canadian women, attracted the leaders of all three major political parties at the time.[7]

NAC believed strongly in the importance of institutional reform, and assumed important roles in the campaigns to include women's equality language in the 1982 Canadian Charter of Rights and Freedoms, and to establish a federally funded Court Challenges Program that would breathe life into new constitutional language. The organization mounted an active issue-based lobby on Parliament Hill.

NAC shifted away from its initial parliamentary focus after 1984, and became increasingly embattled from within and without. As a result, the larger push for mainstream political voice that was embedded in the royal commission report was consigned to a distant back burner. This issue returned to the limelight from time to time thanks to the efforts either of women's groups within political parties, or of cross-party campaigners who were based in cities around the country. As I point out in Chapter 6, organizations like Equal Voice (founded in 2001 in Toronto) have played a crucial role in trying to keep the focus on women's participation and representation, but lack the budget, legitimacy, or public clout that NAC wielded during its early years.

The 1984 federal elections brought to power a 211-seat Progressive Conservative majority government. As the divergence became clearer between where that government wanted to lead Canada and where NAC's leaders wanted the country to go, the group's estrangement from mainstream parliamentary politics only sharpened. By the late 1980s, NAC had assumed a highly critical and largely extraparliamentary opposition role that challenged Tory constitutional plans as well as Prime Minister Brian Mulroney's push for a Canada–United States free trade deal.

NAC suffered a major loss of federal government funding during this period, which was a significant blow because about two-thirds of the organization's annual budget then came from federal sources. Other women's organizations came under the knife as well, as federal

Tories lashed out at groups that were critical of their key policy directions. The Conservatives sliced NAC's federal subsidy by more than half, from about $680,000 to just $300,000, cut $1.6 million from the budget of the Secretary of State Women's Program that funded research and advocacy work, and also eliminated the $2.75 million Court Challenges Program that underwrote the costs of equality litigation using the Charter of Rights and Freedoms.[8]

As if these problems were not enough, NAC was increasingly fractured by intense internal struggles. Women were and remain an enormously diverse group within the population of Canada, spread across all the categories of language, region, ideology, class, sexual orientation, race, rural or urban location, age, and so on, which also divide men. When it came to constitutional questions, for example, Quebec feminists tended to diverge from those in the rest of Canada. NAC leaders found it impossible to reconcile the former's preferences for sovereignty or decentralized federalism with the latter's demands for a strong federal government that could enforce firm national standards in areas such as health care.

There were many other sources of tension. From time to time, lesbian activists claimed the group was dominated by straight women, while in the late 1980s and following, immigrant and visible minority women pressed the organization to abandon what they viewed as white hegemony in favour of anti-racist feminism. Each of these claims reflected a significant and highly defensible argument for better representation inside what was effectively a volunteer-based national umbrella organization. The problem is that each internal upheaval ran the risk of turning women's movement campaigners against each other during a period when the real enemies, so to speak, stood outside the tent.

Observers could be forgiven for wondering whether the major obstacles on the road to equality were the straight, white, English-Canadian activists who'd led NAC, or the Mulroney-era ministers who were chopping support for women's programs.

These powerful internal plus external challenges produced a precipitous decline in NAC's organizational base as well as its public profile. From a high of roughly 586 member groups with 5 million affiliated women in 1988, NAC claimed fewer than 300 member groups by 2005.[9] No NAC president after Judy Rebick, whose term ended in 1993, could claim a level of public recognition such that her name was easily identified by my Canadian politics undergraduate students, let alone by members of the general public. The downward spiral continued, as NAC lost its office space in Toronto and Ottawa, hosted outdated websites, and took on a six-figure debt load.[10]

Above all, once an organized countermovement sprang up, composed of socially conservative women who said feminism did not speak for them, the situation became even more difficult. Even if NAC had remained an effective group that was committed to improving female public representation, it was no longer able to assert uncontested claims on behalf of the women of Canada. The anti-feminist group known as REAL Women (standing for "Realistic, Equal, Active, for Life") emerged on the political scene in the mid-1980s, attracting considerable media interest and cultivating support among Tory MPs and cabinet ministers in Ottawa. The reality of an anti-feminist presence at the federal level was apparent by 1989, when REAL Women received public funding for a conference, just as NAC's support from federal sources was dramatically reduced and the Mulroney Conservatives refused to participate in lobbying sessions with the group.[11]

What remains intriguing about REAL Women and other organizations on the social right is that even as they vigorously denied the public legitimacy of their opponents, they avoided disclosing their own credentials. Who did REAL Women represent? How many women paid annual membership dues to REAL Women? What sources, other than the federal government, funded the operations of the group? When, if at all, were its leaders elected? As long as the membership size, funding sources, and internal organization of REAL Women remained indeterminate, the group seemed even more shadowy and ominous than its core positions—that asserted the patriarchal heterosexual unit was the only legitimate family model, opposed women's reproductive freedom, and routinely condemned pro-equality decisions by Canadian judges.[12]

Anyone who expected NAC to bounce back into the parliamentary limelight once the Liberals returned to power in Ottawa was sorely disappointed in 1993 and following. Under a series of majority (primarily under Jean Chrétien) and minority (under Paul Martin) governments, federal subsidies to NAC dropped to the point that the group became effectively defunct. Moreover, in 1993 and following, the Liberals overhauled the social policy portfolio with which the Conservatives had begun to tinker. The Grits not only dramatically cut transfers to the provinces, but also imposed fixed limits on them and loosened the terms under which provinces spent federal dollars. The reaction of provincial governments stung by these changes was swift and decisive: many chopped their budgets in a major way, offloaded expensive redistributive programs onto the shoulders of municipalities, and generally hunkered down for an extended period of conflict with the feds.

Canadians on the progressive side of the ledger faced an exponentially larger challenge in the wake of these changes.

Every subnational government in the country began looking for ways to save money. For the most part, extra-parliamentary campaigners devoted their energies to fighting either for organizational survival, or for anti-globalization causes that seemed far removed from the here-and-now of domestic public policy.

Even worse, momentum in the House of Commons rested with right-wing interests that fundamentally approved of what the Liberals had done, and that consistently opposed older parliamentary representation arguments voiced by NAC during the 1970s and 1980s. In fact, the rise of the Reform, Alliance, and merged Conservative parties in 1993 and following provided not only a welcome mat, but also a parliamentary home for anti-feminist ideas—including the anti-abortion, pro-patriarchal family, and anti-homosexual positions emanating from the Christian Right in the United States, among others.

The relative weakness of evangelical and fundamen-talist religion in Canada acted to some degree as a brake on these ideas. The 2006 elections, however, brought to Ottawa a Conservative minority government led by Stephen Harper, which was closer to organized anti-feminism than any regime in the country's history.[13] We know that much of the damage to health, welfare, and education programs had been inflicted by the Liberals—who were hardly beacons of hope anyway in 2006, as they limped about in the aftermath of the Quebec sponsorship scandal. This meant many voters (more men that women, it should be noted) believed by 2006 that little differenti-ated the two leading federal parties. Yet female voters seemed to recognize at a visceral level that when it came to women's lives, the Conservative victory entailed far more than a perfunctory changing of the guard on Parliament Hill.

What was it about the 2006 elections that made such a difference, both to the discrediting of basic democratic principles that were crucial to women's engagement, and to the resurgence of older notions of a private female sphere? At its core, Harper's victory provided an authoritative stamp of approval for a party that nominated and elected very few women candidates and MPs, and believed there was absolutely nothing wrong with that scenario. Apart from everything else those facts meant, they spoke volumes about just how marginalized basic claims for enhancing women's participation and representation had become.

Moreover, Harper's inner circle was dominated by committed critics of pro-equality court decisions that had been rendered since 1985, when the equality language in sections 15 and 28 of the Charter of Rights and Freedoms came into effect. Assisted by a close-knit cabal of socially conservative advisors, the new prime minister set his sights on altering the federal judiciary, bureaucracy, and budget in such a way as to undermine progressive gains, prevent future ones, and, broadly speaking, not alarm Canadians about what the new elites were doing in Ottawa.

Federal funding for pro-equality court interventions had been vulnerable in Canada since the early 1990s, only a few years after constitutional equality provisions came into effect. Yet Harper and his team wanted to close the taps on equality even further. They set in motion procedures that altered the way federal judges were appointed, cut funds for a few remaining women's units, and generally pushed the already precarious women's equality locomotive right off the tracks.

What's intriguing about these changes is that the general public in Canada were by no means clamouring for them. Nor did the Harper Conservatives campaign in an upfront way that revealed their socially regressive intentions to the electorate at large. Instead, they marched toward the middle of the spectrum using cautious rhetoric that didn't set off seismic tremors, and then packaged each decision in sanitized wrapping so no one but the true believers who endorsed their actions would even notice.

Altogether, the directions of the Harper government severely compromised the ability of Canadians who cared about women's political involvement to make their case.

Revenge of the Social Conservatives

Elected in 2006, the Harper Conservative caucus included only 14 women out of 127 members (11 percent), compared with 34 women out of 135 members (25 percent) in the governing Liberal caucus in the previous Parliament. Harper appointed only six female ministers to his 26-member first cabinet, three of whom were demoted by the time he shuffled the political executive in the summer of 2007.[14] At that point, the prime minister named five women to his 26-seat cabinet (19 percent). In response to criticism from Equal Voice and other groups, these numbers increased to 11 women in an enlarged 38-member cabinet following the 2008 election. Yet as in 2006, none of them held top positions comparable to those held by women of the Mulroney years and following, such as deputy prime minister, minister of foreign affairs, or minister of justice.

These patterns are rather eye-popping, in the sense that they reflect limited progress relative to the previous Liberal regime and the records set by the Progressive Conservatives during the 1980s. Brian Mulroney appointed six women to his 29-member cabinet in 1984, and was the first prime minister to offer them senior posts including foreign affairs, justice, and defence. In addition, Mulroney spoke openly about his efforts to recruit more women to run for federal seats, and about his party's plans to press the chartered banks to lend more money to female entrepreneurs.

In an interview with journalist Sydney Sharpe, Mulroney described himself as "a one-man affirmative action course" after he'd been tutored by Tory women.[15] This was more than mere hot air. The Progressive Conservatives fielded 23 female candidates federally in 1984, or 8.1 percent of their total, and then 37 women or 12.5 percent in 1988.[16] Although their numbers in both years fell considerably short of comparable figures for the Liberals and especially for the New Democrats, the PCs in 1988 were slightly ahead of where their successors in the merged Conservative organization would be 20 years later.

In 2006, Harper's field of 308 federal candidates included 38 women, or 12.3 percent of the Tory total. His numbers in 2004 were 36, or 11.6 percent of the Conservative total. These levels not only fell short of Progressive Conservative numbers in the late Mulroney period, but also looked miniscule relative to those of the Liberals, NDP, and Bloc Québécois. Average percentages of women candidates fielded in 2004 and 2006 were 25 percent for the Liberals, 33 percent for the NDP, and 27 percent for the BQ.[17]

Given this background, it's not surprising that more than 40 percent of the federal NDP caucus (12 out of 29) in 2007 was female, as was 21 percent of the Liberal Official Opposition (21 out of 101) and 33 percent of the BQ caucus (17 out of 51). On the government side, the level rested at 11 percent (14 out of 125), which reflected the logical flow-through from relatively low numbers of Conservative women candidates who contested election in the first place. As a result, Stephen Harper did not have a deep bench of women in the Commons from whom to recruit cabinet members, even though the television shots may have given a different impression. About half the women in his caucus sat strategically positioned around him so it looked like the Tory benches were evenly split between the genders.

These low numbers of female candidates, caucus members, and ministers did not appear to worry Canada's governing party, however. Speaking in the summer of 2007, senior Conservatives stuck by their well-rehearsed argument that capable individuals always rise to the top, meaning no interventions were necessary to encourage, recruit, or (heaven forbid) appoint women as legislative candidates. In fact, when asked why so few females had been named to Harper's 2007 cabinet, a top Tory turned the question around in such a way as to suggest that women in Canada were themselves the problem. According to a Canadian Press story that appeared on August 15,

> One of the women just named to a junior ministerial role defended her party's reluctance to hand-pick female candidates and preference for an open, democratic process. Diane Ablonczy says women who enter politics generally have even more opportunities than men, because leaders want to promote women to prominent positions. But the reality, she says, is that women are generally less interested in political careers. "Women generally place a higher priority on caring for their family—either their own children, or sometimes grandchildren, and sometimes older parents," Ablonczy said in an interview. "It's not a career choice that a lot of women make."[18]

The message from Ablonczy, who ran in 2002 for the Alliance leadership and was responsible for introducing the prime minister to his wife Laureen, appeared to blame Canadian women for being consumed by apolitical priorities.

Ablonczy's statement struck me as rather disingenuous. Here was a senior Conservative woman, on the outer fringe of the federal cabinet, ascribing the absence of women in politics to a diversion that the social right in her own party had warmly and passionately championed—namely, caring for other family members. The fact that these so-called family values ideas conflicted with recruiting more women to public life never seemed to dawn on Ablonczy, nor on the journalists who interviewed her. Moreover, the view she expressed in 2007 directly contradicted a perspective she offered only five years earlier, in the midst of the Alliance leadership campaign against Harper. At that time, Ablonczy suggested discriminatory attitudes rather than freely made individual choices constituted a major brake against women's political mobility. In 2002, she told a reporter for the *Edmonton Journal* that "Some people in the Alliance are asking if a female leader could have the strength and vision and determination…to lead the party …I do think people still tend to think of leaders more in the male context."[19]

Ablonczy's 2007 comments are also intriguing given the heightened care-giving burdens shouldered by individual women as well as men since the federal government began shredding social programs during the Mulroney years. From this standpoint, the sustained attention that Canadians devoted to their families had a great deal to do with the absence of robust national health care (especially home care and elder care), social assistance, and education provisions (including care for young children). Moreover, if average citizens were avoiding politics, that aversion was entirely understandable given the drumbeat heard from the right since the 1970s that said only markets mattered, while the state was largely irrelevant.[20] For both reasons, the story behind Ablonczy's comments struck me as being more about constraints placed on individuals by the country's policy makers than about free choices available to women citizens.

Even a cursory look at poll data since Harper's election as leader of the merged Conservative party shows that women in the general public were far from enamoured with him. His weaker standing among females compared to males, referred to as the "gender gap," was considerable, meaning many women in Canada spoke with their feet when it came to engagement with the Conservatives. During the 2004 election campaign, Ipsos-Reid polls showed Harper gained among men but not women, to the point that he was ten percentage points weaker among females (at 26 percent) than males (at 36 percent) in early June of that year.[21]

Male voters again warmed up to Harper during the 2006 election campaign, while women did not. Moreover, female voters were less likely to support issue positions associated with the Conservative party that year. These included claims that the Liberals were corrupt, that same-sex marriage should be opposed, that the federal gun registry should be scrapped, and that private hospitals should be allowed in Canada.[22]

In fact, poll numbers reported in June 2004 hardly budged at all during the next few years. A Strategic Counsel study in July 2007 reported Conservative support still at 26 percent among women, and at 37 percent among men. As in earlier years, issue positions helped to underpin this difference, with women in 2007 far less willing than men to endorse Canada's mission in Afghanistan.[23] Unlike the patterns in 2004 and 2006, when the NDP tended to benefit from women's support, 2007 data showed the Liberals' standing was almost the reverse to that of the Tories, with Grit support at 36 percent among women and 27 percent among men. Data from 2008 revealed the governing Conservative party stuck at 26 percent among Canadian women.[24]

The Harper Conservatives tried to avoid highly charged issues like abortion during their election campaigns and first two years in power, although one government MP did introduce legislation in March 2008 that would criminalize the act of harming a fetus. Moreover, social right allies of the Harper government embarked on a campaign during the summer of 2008 to discredit Supreme Court of Canada Chief Justice Beverley McLachlin, on the grounds that she ostensibly played a role in approving the appointment of abortion rights advocate Dr. Henry Morgentaler to the Order of Canada. It seemed that as cautious and restrained as they made themselves out to be, Conservatives were still pursuing an anti-equality agenda, and were perceived by many Canadian women as less moderate than their window-dressing suggested. Despite what was said for public consumption, the governing party evoked a visceral sense that suspicion, if not outright disbelief, was warranted.

This was, after all the same political party that opposed public child-care programs, and that effectively demolished the nascent national child-care scheme that was emerging during the Paul Martin government of 2004 and following. Conservatives endorsed care by mothers for their own children in their own homes as the best model for the country, and introduced a targeted tax allowance for that purpose in 2006. Stephen Harper did not need to get up on a soapbox to trash working mothers, celebrate patriarchy, or tell Canadians the end of the world was nigh if children went to public daycare centres. All he had to do was stop the progress then underway toward a national system and bring in the tax change, and the rest—for anyone who cared to read the tea leaves—was understood.

Who cheered the child-care decision? Well, REAL Women was delighted, and offered not only to help develop the fiscal details but also to do "what we can to educate the public and to lay the groundwork for controversy to come when the bill is brought forward."[25] The group issued a press release in the fall of 2006 congratulating the Harper government for facing down what REAL Women vice-president Gwen Landolt termed "the most powerful feminist lobby in the world."[26] Clearly, REAL Women either enjoyed fighting paper tigers or else thrived on imaginative fantasies. As a parliamentary lobby presence, NAC had at that point been sidelined for more than 20 years.

The Tories' $1200 annual allowance for each pre-school child was supplemented in their 2007 budget by a new child tax credit as well as an enriched spousal deduction, designed to advantage households with single—and overwhelmingly male—earners. Again, the cheering section was not hard to identify. Tom Flanagan, an early Reform and later Conservative party insider based in Calgary, waxed ecstatic over policies that "provide modest but real incentives for more of our young people to get married, stay married, have children and invest in their future." He was thrilled to see Martin-era child-care initiatives derailed because they "would pull children out of the home and into the hands of a bureaucratic daycare establishment."[27]

When it came to undermining what was left of a women's unit presence in the federal government, REAL Women was also right there to cheerlead. Harper's heritage minister, Bev Oda, announced in November 2006 that three-quarters of the regional offices of Status of Women Canada would be closed by the spring of 2007, as part of a $5 million cut to that agency's annual budget of $23 million. The notion of fostering equality was summarily stripped from the mandate of the agency. The response of REAL Women? To quote it directly: "This is a good start, and we hope that the Status of Women will eventually be eliminated entirely since it does not represent 'women,' but only represents the ideology of feminists."[28] Whom REAL Women represented was neither revealed nor did Canada's political reporters or commentators pursue the question.

From the perspective of democratic process, however, probably the most significant and dangerous changes introduced by the Harper government involved Canada's courts. In a profoundly important two-pronged action, the Conserv-atives announced in 2006 that they would cut off funds for Charter litigation and also change the way federal judges were selected. REAL Women applauded the decision to wipe out the Court Challenges Program, which the Liberals had reinstated in the mid-1990s after the initiative was cut by the Mulroney government. According to Canada's leading anti-feminist organization, the program "was a profoundly undemocratic use of taxpayers' money to restructure society...The elimination of the Court Challenges Program will go a long way to promoting democracy in Canada."[29]

If there were ever a contest to reward Orwellian double-speak, I'd nominate that statement for top prize. It asserted, somehow, that eliminating the financial supports that permitted disadvantaged groups to realize their own constitutional rights would *improve* Canadian democracy. Volume after volume of liberal political theory (not to mention more radical variants of democratic thought) alongside centuries of experience dating back to the Magna Carta, have posited the opposite—namely, that for polities to realize their full democratic potential, marginalized interests need voices backed up by resources.

The move to eliminate the Court Challenges Program formed only a small part, however, of a much larger and longer-term campaign by proponents of the so-called "Calgary School" to transform Canada's judiciary. Arguing since the dawn of Charter litigation that Canadian judges wrongly sided with equality-seeking claimants (notably women's groups, lesbian and gay organizations, and others with whom they disagreed), right-wing academics including Tom Flanagan and Ian Brodie pledged to alter the bench's directions once their protégé, Stephen Harper, was installed in the Prime Minister's Office.[30]

This cabal got to work immediately after the January 2006 elections, using Brodie's position as chief of staff to Harper to ensure the roll-out was smooth and effective. In February, the prime minister announced his Supreme Court nominee would face questions from MPs in front of TV cameras, as part of setting in place the groundwork for major changes to Canadian judicial appointments. In September, Harper named David Brown to the Ontario Superior Court. Brown's appointment raised many eyebrows, given that he had served as counsel to REAL Women and other social conservative interests in their efforts to roll back abortion rights, block same-sex marriage, and generally defend positions associated with the religious right.[31] A parade of similar nominees to the bench continued unabated, as Harper stacked judicial appointment advisory committees with like-minded folks—meaning they shared the Calgary School world view about which Canadians did and which did not deserve to have their rights considered in a court of law.[32]

The secretive organization known as REAL Women expressed consistent delight with the directions of the

Harper government.[33] Yet, as an organization of indeterminate size, composition, and representativeness, REAL Women likely spoke for only a small fraction of the minority of adult females who supported Tory candidates in 2006. For women voters generally in Canada, only about a quarter of whom *chose* the Harper Conservatives as their government, things looked far from rosy: A top Conservative blamed women as a group for not getting involved in parliamentary politics, even though the ideological push from her side of the spectrum led precisely in the direction of keeping them at home. There, as the party brain trust and its REAL Women allies prescribed, they could remain properly married wives and mothers, busily engaged in the work of caring for others.

Without disclosing whence it drew its members or funding, Canada's leading anti-feminist group managed to cultivate a compellingly authoritative voice. Who elected REAL Women, after all? Was there any possibility of asserting a collective countervoice that would challenge its narrow, socially conservative view? Where were the opportunities to re-inject mainstream politics with a sense of civic dynamism, in which the values of equality, participation, and democracy as understood by moderate Canadians, would take primacy? We take up these key questions in Chapter 6.

Notes

1. Thatcher as quoted in Wendy Webster. *Not a Man to Match her: The Marketing of a Prime Minister* (London: Women's Press, 1990), 57.
2. Margaret Thatcher, *The Downing Street Years* (New York: HarperCollins, 1993), 146–147.

3. See http://www.elections.ca/content.asp?section=pas&docu ment=turnout&lang=e&textonly=false, consulted 25 September 2007.

4. See Naomi Klein, *No Logo: Taking Aim at the Brand Bullies* (Toronto: Knopf, 2000); Naomi Klein, *The Shock Doctrine: The Rise of Disaster Capitalism* (Toronto: Knopf, 2007).

5. Susan Faludi, *Backlash: The Undeclared War Against American Women* (New York: Doubleday, 1991).

6. On the role of social conservatism in marginalizing women in US politics, see Sue Thomas and Jean Reith Schroedel, "The Significance of Social and Institutional Expectations," in Lori Cox Han and Caroline Heldman, eds., *Rethinking Madam President* (Boulder, Colorado: Lynne Rienner, 2007), 50–55.

7. On NAC's early engagement with parliamentary politics, see Jill Vickers, Pauline Rankin, and Christine Appelle, *Politics as if Women Mattered: A Political Analysis of the National Action Committee on the Status of Women* (Toronto: University of Toronto Press, 1993); Lisa Young, *Feminists and Party Politics* (Vancouver: UBC Press, 2000).

8. See Sylvia Bashevkin, *Women on the Defensive: Living Through Conservative Times* (Toronto: University of Toronto Press, 1998), 124, 126.

9. These membership data are drawn from Bashevkin, *Women on the Defensive*, 39; and from Naomi Black, "Broccoli or Spinach? Studying the Women's Movement in Canada and Elsewhere." Paper delivered at the American Political Science Association meetings, Chicago, 2007.

10. See http://en.wikipedia.org/wiki/National_Action_Committee _on_the_Status_of_Women, consulted 7 September 2007. NAC's own English language website listed no news coverage of the organization since 2001. See http://www.nac-cca.ca/ about/news_e.htm, consulted 7 September 2007.

11. See Sylvia Bashevkin, *Toeing the Lines: Women and Party Politics in English Canada*, 2nd ed., (Toronto: Oxford University Press, 1993), 38–39.

12. See http://www.realwomenca.com/about.htm, consulted 25 September 2007.

13. See Marci McDonald, "Stephen Harper and the Theo-cons," *The Walrus* (October 2006), 45–61.

14. The three ministers were Rona Ambrose and Bev Oda, both demoted to lesser positions in the cabinet, and Carol Skelton, who was dropped from the summer 2007 cabinet after announcing she would not seek re-election.

15. Mulroney as quoted in Sydney Sharpe, *The Gilded Ghetto: Women and Political Power in Canada* (Toronto: HarperCollins, 1994), 114–115.

16. See Bashevkin, *Toeing the Lines*, 2nd ed., 83.

17. In 2006, the Liberals and NDP fielded 79 and 108 female candidates respectively, from a total of 308, while the BQ fielded 23 out of 75. In 2004, the Liberals and NDP fielded 75 and 96 women respectively, again from 308, while the BQ ran 18 out of 75.

18. Ablonczy as quoted in Alexander Panetta, "Harper Presents Third-Straight Cabinet Without any Women in Senior Posts," Canadian Press story posted at http://www.recorder.ca/cp/National/070815/n0815146A.html, consulted 26 September 2007.

19. Ablonczy as quoted in Linda Trimble and Jane Arscott, *Still Counting: Women in Politics Across Canada* (Peterborough: Broadview, 2003), 97.

20. See Olena Hankivsky, *Social Policy and the Ethic of Care* (Vancouver: UBC Press, 2004); Paul Kershaw, *Carefair: Rethinking the Responsibilities and Rights of Citizenship* (Vancouver: UBC Press, 2005).

21. Drew Fagan, "Voters Don't Trust Liberals, Pollster Says," *The Globe and Mail* (5 June 2004).

22. Elisabeth Gidengil, Joanna Everitt, Neil Nevitte, André Blais, and Patrick Fournier, "Women to the Left, Men to the Right," *The Globe and Mail* (15 February 2006), A15.

23. Brian Laghi, "Harper Failing to Win Country Over," *The Globe and Mail* (19 July 2007), A1.

24. Nanos Research data reported in Jeffrey Simpson, "Why the Conservatives Haven't Closed the Gender Gap," *The Globe and Mail* (15 February 2008), A19. See also Erin Anderssen,

"Why Do Women Resist this Face?" *The Globe and Mail* (29 March 2008), F6; and Lawrence Martin, "A Party for Women, a Party for Men?" *The Globe and Mail* (9 June 2008), A15.

25. Gwen Landolt, vice-president of REAL Women, quoted in Brian Laghi, "Social Conservatives to Sell Tory Daycare Plan," *The Globe and Mail* (19 April 2006), A1.

26. Charlie Smith, "Women Kick Harper's Ass," *Georgia Straight* (14–21 December 2006), 47.

27. Tom Flanagan, "Family Tax Breaks: Give Credit Where Credit is Due," *The Globe and Mail* (26 March 2007), A13.

28. REAL Women official statement, as quoted in Charlie Smith, "Women Kick Harper's Ass."

29. REAL Women, press release dated 26 September 2006, as quoted in Charlie Smith, "Women Kick." The decision to eliminate the Court Challenges Program was addressed in a December 2007 Federal Court application by a coalition of pro-equality groups.

30. On relations among Flanagan, Brodie, Harper and others, see John Ibbitson, "Educating Stephen," *The Globe and Mail* (26 June 2004), F4–5.

31. See Kirk Makin, "PM's Pick for Bench Draws Fire," *The Globe and Mail* (21 September 2006), A5.

32. See Campbell Clark, "Partisans Filling Judge Nomination Committees," *The Globe and Mail* (12 February 2007), A1; Christin Schmitz, "Conservatives Aim to Replace Judicial 'Charterphiles' with 'Charterphobes?' *The Lawyers Weekly* 27:18 (14 September 2007). This politicization of the judiciary continued apace with a Conservative decision in summer 2008 to appoint two cabinet ministers to the Supreme Court appointment advisory panel.

33. In the spring of 2008, REAL Women announced its support for Conservative government efforts to deny tax credits for ostensibly offensive television and film productions. See Gloria Galloway, "REAL Women Back Film Tax Measures," *The Globe and Mail* (10 April 2008), A7.

~ 6 ~

What To Do

How can we reverse the *women plus power equals discomfort* equation, not only to create more ease for the current cohort of female politicians but also to encourage new participants to engage at all levels?

This chapter proposes eight specific initiatives to improve the treatment of individuals who are already active in political life, and to increase the supply of and demand for new talent. Coming out of the material presented in Chapter 5, it addresses the larger climate surrounding public citizenship, arguing that without a systematic revaluing of mainstream involvement, few creative or energetic people will want to get involved in formal politics at any level.

In order to make things better, we can pursue any number of different strategies. They include formal, rule-based challenges to the status quo that could, for example, require all eligible voters to vote in elections, or create legislated quotas under which parties would need to field minimum percentages of women candidates. Another avenue might alter Canada's electoral rules by introducing some element of proportionality to established first-past-the-post rules, in the hopes that electoral system reform would drive up voter turnout and help to elect more women. A fourth option uses the courts or industry complaint mechanisms as vehicles for contesting biased media portrayals of elected officials.

At the other end of the spectrum from these reforms are informal, voluntary approaches that seek to accomplish similar goals using less invasive techniques. Rather than threatening to take media proprietors and their employees to court, for instance, informal strategies would exhort these individuals through the power of persuasion to clean up their act. Instead of setting quotas requiring parties to recruit more female candidates, and having parties risk the loss of public subsidies if they fail to comply, voluntary efforts can try to cajole political leaders to increase their numbers—by using positive incentives rather than negative sanctions.

More than 35 years have elapsed since the 1970 release of the Report of the Royal Commission on the Status of Women, which recommended voluntary strategies. Many subsequent efforts to increase women's participation in Canadian politics, including those pursued by Women for Political Action during the 1970s and the Committee for '94 through 1994, have adopted a similar approach. For the most part, informal efforts have implored, exhorted, and encouraged parties not only to recruit more women to senior posts, but also to offer training and mentorship opportunities for prospective activists and to financially assist women candidates.

In an effort to push beyond this conventional approach and confront power discomforts head on, we begin by considering the four avenues for formal rule change described earlier, most of which have been ignored or dismissed in Canada as too extreme or interventionist: mandatory voting, legislative quotas for female candidates, electoral reform toward greater proportionality, and the use of the courts and press councils to seek more balanced media coverage. In the sections that follow, each of these proposals is evaluated with reference to its ability to focus public attention on obstacles facing women's participation, the likelihood that it will increase citizen engagement in mainstream politics, and the probability that, if introduced, we'd actually see a more gender-balanced elite.

The chapter then maps out a number of informal options that follow from the last five chapters, arguing that a concerted push on the voluntary side—backed up by the revaluation of public life and the threat of more formal sanctions—could go a long way toward heightening comfort levels for women and other traditionally marginalized groups in politics. Informal strategies outlined here include:

- re-invigorating a parliamentary-focused feminist movement
- systematically monitoring the media treatment of female politicians
- sustained probing of the representational claims of organized anti-feminism
- getting involved in politics, and joining groups like Equal Voice that work to keep women's participation on the public agenda

Each of these informal avenues is far less complicated, and far more doable, than the formal change proposals suggested in the next section. Yet, taken together, they could potentially revolutionize Canadian politics by raising the voices of the 52 percent of the population that have hardly been heard in recent years.

Changing the Rules of the Game
Proposal 1: Mandatory Voting

Attracting more participants to mainstream politics is far from simple in an age when formal institutional engagement has been made to seem irrelevant. For decades, as argued in Chapter 5, the political right has relegated government to a secondary position behind the market-place. At the same time, the extraparliamentary left has projected a similar view by directing protest toward global capitalism rather than the nation-state. Voter turnout in Canada and elsewhere has declined, as has public trust in the politicians who are elected by increasingly smaller fractions of the citizenry.

We need to revalue citizen participation as crucial to the democratic life of Canada, including each of its provinces, territories, and local governments. What better way to get more people involved than to rank the baseline exercise of citizen voice on the same level as other acts that we expect of each other? Each of us is required by law to file an income tax return if we have taxable income. If our name is selected, we must make ourselves available to serve on a jury for a civil or criminal case. After the tragic outbreak of SARS in Toronto, every person entering a hospital or other health-care facility in Canada's largest city was expected to use antibacterial hand wash.

Voting in elections should be at least as important as filing an income tax return, serving on a jury, or preventing the spread of disease. Each of these tasks, including voting, shares an integral sense of individual responsibility for a larger collective. We can't shrug off paying taxes even if it rains or snows on the deadline of April 30. Nor do we permit people to shirk jury duty simply because they don't like the lawyers, judge, or parties to a case who appear at their assigned trial. And it was impossible to refuse to use the antibacterial dispenser on entering a hospital on the basis that the soap didn't smell good or we were running late.

A clear way to revalue political citizenship, and renew public interest in formal institutional engagement, is to introduce compulsory voting to Canada. Voting has long been mandatory in a number of other democratic systems, including Australia since 1924 and Belgium since 1892.[1] The penalties for failing to vote in countries with such a law differ widely, and are enforced to various degrees, but the general pattern of effectiveness is clear. Systems with compulsory voting, or with a history of mandatory voting laws in at least some jurisdictions, tend to have higher rates of voter turnout than those without that mechanism. One comprehensive study of participation across Western Europe, conducted for the respected International Institute for Democracy and Electoral Assistance (IDEA), showed average rates of turnout in elections since 1945 were highest (above 90 percent) in four countries with a history of compulsory voting—Belgium, Austria, Italy, and Luxembourg.[2]

Let's focus on Australia, a place with parliamentary and federal systems similar to those in Canada. Both countries strongly value individual rights and the Westminster-style traditions of a constitutional monarchy. Longitudinal research reveals that Australia placed 16th in voter turnout in an international ranking of 172 democracies, with an average turnout of 84.4 percent in 21 federal elections since 1945. In contrast, Canada placed 77th, with average turnout at 68.4 percent in 17 post–World War II elections.[3] In the fall 2007 election in Ontario, turnout dropped to a record low of just over 50 percent.[4]

Critics of mandatory voting are quick to argue that forcing citizens to vote violates individual freedoms. Yet in Anglo-American systems like Australia's, individual rights are clearly protected because the ballot remains secret and there are multiple options, including those for reluctant voters. People who don't like the choices on offer can spoil their ballots, vote for a random candidate, or simply leave the form blank by not marking an "X" anywhere. Even within Canada, we have not to this point seen a successful court challenge to tax laws, jury duty, or hospital hand-washing rules, each of which is arguably an infringement on purist concepts of individual liberty. So, for that matter, are laws restricting alcohol consumption in public places, limiting the age at which alcohol can be purchased, requiring children to attend school, and imposing speed limits and driver licensing provisions.

Rather than focusing on these rights infringement arguments, I would suggest that the benefits of compulsory voting outweigh the disadvantages. Getting more citizens to vote would bring Canadian democracy closer to the *sine qua non* of a model polity—namely, government by all the people, rather than by the slim majority of adults who presently get themselves to polling stations on election day. Requiring citizens to vote might also have an educational effect, in that it would encourage more Canadians to find out about the parties, candidates, issues, and broader election practices that shape our lives. Putting in place a law that makes voting mandatory will hopefully stimulate not just curiosity about mainstream political institutions, but also engagement with those structures.

Two useful parallel examples to this argument involve liquor laws and driver licensing practices. Adolescents may not be enamoured with controls on who can buy beer and spirits, or when or where, or how many levels of driver testing they must pass in order to acquire full certification. Despite their lack of enthusiasm, however, most young people learn the rules of the game, figure out how best to navigate the system, and follow the law at an impressionable stage of their lives. It seems more than appropriate to set in place a similar developmental process for learning about democracy, which should rank as at least as significant to Canadian society as absorbing norms about responsible drinking and careful driving.

By increasing citizen involvement, we would enhance the legitimacy of our democracy. Federal and provincial governments that win power based on voter turnouts around 60 percent clearly do not have sweeping public mandates, even though they frequently operate as if they do. In a typical federal or provincial Canadian election, where three or more candidates run in each constituency, 40 percent of the popular vote is usually enough for a party to win the most seats and form a government. If only 60 percent of the eligible voters actually vote, a mere 24 percent of the adult citizens will have voted for the winning party. This is hardly a solid popular foundation, but it exceeds the support, for example, of the federal Liberals in 2004. That year, Paul Martin won a minority government with 36.7 percent of the popular vote, with turnout around 61 percent.

Participation in Canadian elections is even lower at the local level, where mayors, members of city councils, and school board trustees face a pool of active voters that constitutes only a minority of the eligible adult population. In Ontario, the 1994 average turnout in cities of 100,000 or more was just 37 percent. In Toronto's 2003 and 2006 municipal elections, roughly 40 percent of eligible voters chose the mayor and councillors who would govern the largest city in the country.[5] French school board elections in Quebec drew only 8 percent of eligible voters in 2003, while English school board elections attracted 15 percent that year.[6] The turnout in Vancouver municipal elections in 2005 was 32 percent.[7]

In short, contemporary patterns of voter turnout in Canada translate into fairly shallow foundations for democratic government—especially at the local level. The core contribution of compulsory voting, whether at the federal, provincial, or local level, would not be to create onerous sanctions or enforcement, since comparative research shows these hardly make much difference to turnout levels. Instead, by offering clear evidence that we value public participation as a fundamental individual responsibility, mandatory voting could go a long way toward getting more citizens engaged in the crucial act of choosing our public leaders.

Proposal 2: Legislative Quotas

The issue of democratic legitimacy also underpins arguments for legislative quotas, which would require parties to nominate fixed proportions of candidates from designated groups, whether women, sexual minorities, youth, aboriginals, or ethno-cultural minorities. Quotas can be imposed via constitutional entrenchment, through legislation, or internally by parties themselves. Thus far, only the NDP has adopted internal quotas; no constitutional or legislative channels have yet been pursued for this purpose in Canada.

Moreover, consistent with Italian political scientist Licia Papavero's findings, the NDP's policy did not spill over into other parts of the political spectrum.[8] The fact that the party adopted an affirmative action policy in 1991, which stated that the party would run women candidates in 50 percent of federal constituencies (including a minimum of 60 percent females in winnable seats without NDP incumbents) helps to explain the strong representation of women in the party caucus.[9] As data presented in Chapter 5 show, the fact that the NDP in 2006 surpassed 40 percent women in the party's House of Commons caucus not only broke its own records, but also far eclipsed comparable figures for other federal parties.

Typically, candidate quotas are introduced in order to raise the numbers of politicians from traditionally marginalized groups. Going back to arguments about representation that we discussed in Chapter 1, their purpose is to ensure legislators more closely mirror the public at large—whether for symbolic, policy-related, or basic political justice reasons. The assumption behind quota proposals is that since electors grant legitimacy to the elected, the two must be reasonably similar in demographic terms.

Canadians hold this view very dear when it comes to geographical representation. Perhaps because Canada is so large in terms of territory, and because the stark northern landscape of trees, rocks, and wilderness has long stood as a defining feature of our art and literature, political entities in this country are closely structured around categories of physical space. We comfortably speak of provinces, local constituencies, city wards, and neighbourhood precincts.

We are far less comfortable, however, with notions of people-based demographic categories, whether grounded in such identities as social class, ethnicity, or gender. In the ideal world we envisage from our individualistic starting points, gender quota rules should not be necessary. Women will make their way upward through existing recruitment channels, just like men do. If they can't, then perhaps they just need to try harder.

A different approach to the stagnant or declining numbers of women in Canadian politics says trying harder is not the answer. In fact, working harder to get to the top has been the main strategy chosen by campaigners in this area since the 1970s, and it hasn't produced measurable advances for the past 15 years. Perhaps we need to try working smarter, rather than harder, using existing geographic quotas in Canada as a guide. What about introducing rules that insist on gender representation—to parallel existing provisions that entrench geographic or territorial quotas in our system?

"What territorial quotas?" you might ask. The British North America Act of 1867 gave us clear constitutional provisions governing the numbers of senators and MPs from various provinces. Canada's original constitution doesn't use the term "quotas" in referring to these rules, and we don't commonly refer to them as such, but that's effectively what they are. In paragraphs called "Representation of the provinces in the Senate" and "Electoral districts of the four provinces," the BNA Act stipulated precisely how many members from Ontario, Quebec, Nova Scotia, and New Brunswick would be appointed to the Senate or elected to the House of Commons.[10] As additional provinces and territories joined Confederation, and as the population of the country increased, successive iterations of the 1867 text laid out revised terms of representation in both houses of Parliament.[11]

As research by Choudhry and Pal has shown, rigid understandings of land representation have poorly served recent generations of immigrants to Canada, many of whom settled in major cities in Ontario, British Columbia, and Alberta. The number of voters per constituency in our urban centres far outweighs the ratio prevailing in small towns and rural areas, making it exceptionally hard to defend the fairness of our electoral system for new citizens of the Canadian polity.[12] Women in diverse ethno-cultural communities thus carry a triple disadvantage from their positions as women, multicultural citizens, and typically, highly under-represented urban voters.

This history helps to explain why constitutional language entrenching gender quotas tends to be found in emergent or developing democracies, rather than older, established ones. It is much easier to insert innovative ideas during the formative stages of building a new, fluid document than it is to revisit the terms of an aged arrangement. As Canadians, we have only to recall the rancour over the Meech Lake and Charlottetown accords to be reminded of how hard it is to alter an existing constitutional deal.

One widely cited instance in which gender quotas were successfully introduced to a nascent system comes from Rwanda. There, a post-genocide constitution reserved at least 30 percent of all government positions for females. In the 2003 elections, women won nearly 50 percent of the seats in Rwanda's new legislature, which meant the quota of at least 30 percent operated as a floor or foundation, rather than as a ceiling or barrier, for higher numbers.

Constitutional quotas have been less effective in more fixed environments, including France. A 1999 constitutional amendment known as the "parity law" required parties to field at least 50 percent female candidates, and specified the terms under which public subsidies would be reduced for organizations that failed to uphold this rule. Given that the language of the parity law was loose—for example, it permitted parties to run women in unwinnable seats, and allowed those that fielded no female candidates whatsoever to still obtain half their state funding—the change had limited effect on representation in the National Assembly. France's standing in an international ranking of proportions of women members in lower parliamentary houses actually dropped after the reform was introduced, from 59th to 61st place.[13]

In the middle ground, between constitutional provisions and voluntary internal rules adopted by a single party, are candidate quota laws that set out a required percentage of legislative candidates. These laws have been introduced in several democratic systems; some newer, such as Argentina and Iraq, and some older, such as Belgium and Costa Rica. In Belgium, the 1994 Electoral Act said that no more than two-thirds of the candidates on any party list for the 1999 elections could be of the same sex. This provision applied to all elections in the country, from sub-national municipal councils to supra-national votes for the European Parliament. The penalty for failure to comply? Belgian parties that did not follow the law faced having their full slate of candidates declared invalid.[14]

Clearly, this version of the Belgian legislation is not appropriate at the local level in Canada, where parties are often either not active or not visible to voters, and where women have already reached the one-third level on a number of city councils. The approach is attractive, however, at the provincial and federal levels—particularly if the terms of the legislation were phrased so that no more than 55 or 60 percent of a party's candidates could be of the same sex, and that parties would be rewarded financially if they nominated more than the required base level. Moreover, the Belgian penalty seems worth adopting, since it gets away from the strictly financial sanctions pursued under France's parity law—where parties can make a mockery of women's equality, and retain their "old-boy network" practices, simply by sacrificing part of their public subsidy. In Belgium, risking the invalidation of an entire party's slate of candidates poses a serious choice: either play by the rules, or don't bother playing at all.

No doubt, any proposal for legislative quotas will be widely condemned by conservatives and many centrists across Canada. We are likely to hear shouts of outrage against unnecessary meddling in the internal affairs of proper and upright parties, whose members know best how to recruit candidates and run campaigns in this large and complex country. We will undoubtedly be told that individuals who have earned the confidence of their peers and who merit the privilege of standing for office will make

their way through the current system, and that quota legislation will accomplish absolutely nothing of value because
it is fundamentally undemocratic.

In response to those protestations, let's bear in mind
that existing public finance laws effectively make the
people of Canada major shareholders in the political
parties. As citizens and, yes, as taxpayers, we each have the
right to demand equitable, accountable practices in the
organizations in which we make major investments. In
2004, for instance, public subsidies to federal political
parties included $9.5 million to the Liberals, $8.5 million
to the Conservatives, $2.4 million to the BQ, and $1.9
million to the NDP.[15] Public subsidies are also paid out at
the provincial level, where a system of tax credits (generally
via income tax receipts) works to increase the value of
political contributions to parties. As well, some provinces
have instituted annual allowances to qualifying parties,
alongside reimbursements of election expenses for qualifying candidates.[16]

It's simply not reasonable to say the parties can go about
their business as they see fit while the people of Canada pay
a part of their bills. Legislative quotas would force parties
that do not presently run more than a token handful of
female candidates to sit up and take notice. At the very least,
the proposal that we move in the direction of quotas might
so unnerve enough party recruiters (especially on the right
of the spectrum) that they'd seek out women candidates
more actively than they do presently. If the point of the
exercise is to open up avenues for action, then that's not a
bad outcome.

Gender quota discussions would also spotlight the political representation of other groups. If we're comfortable
with geographic quotas, and we're ready to think about
quotas as a way to increase women's numbers in politics,

then why not consider ways to attract more aboriginal people, youth, members of sexual minorities, and diverse ethno-cultural groups to Canada's legislatures? Given that women are a demographic majority across each of these categories, let's bring on the larger conversation, with the clear recognition that gender must remain an integral part of every discussion of diversifying our public leadership.

Proposal 3: Electoral Reform

Unanimity is a rare commodity in social science research, but just about every comparative study ever published reaches the same conclusion: proportionality in an electoral system is more conducive to women's participation than the single-member-plurality (SMP; also called "first-past-the-post") system used in Canada. This literature strongly suggests that if electoral reform were introduced alongside candidate quotas and mandatory voting, we would soon see far more gender-balanced numbers in all our deliberative bodies, from city councils to provincial legislatures to the House of Commons.[17]

How does proportionality in an electoral system benefit women? Harvard University political scientist Pippa Norris offers one of the clearest explanations of the advantage that accrues under proportionality, and the disadvantage that follows from plurality arrangements:

Under proportional systems, each party presents the voters with a list of candidates in each multimember constituency. To increase votes for the list, parties have an incentive to include candidates representing all major social sectors of the electorate. Excluding any major social group, including women, could signal discrimination, and the group that feels excluded would not vote for that party. By contrast in other electoral systems (called "first past the post," by analogy with a race), each party nominates one parliamentary candidate in each constituency, and the candidate with the most votes wins. Where the selection of candidates is in the hands of the local constituency party organization, this creates minimal incentives for each constituency to pick a ticket that is 'balanced' among different groups at the district or national level. Local party members often want a representative who will maximize their chances of winning in that constituency, irrespective of the broader consequences for the party or parliament.[18]

Given that Canada has one of the world's most decentralized candidate selection systems, we live with the double-whammy effects of the plurality electoral scheme described by Norris, plus an extremely localized sense of who makes a good nominee. With these institutional parameters shaping our polity, it's pretty amazing we've reached even a one-fifth threshold for women MPs.

In recent years, frustration over the imbalance between the percentage of votes received by parties in an election and the proportion of legislative seats they win has bubbled up in several provinces. Typically, plurality systems like ours award more seats to winning parties than their popular vote would predict. At the same time, first-past-the-post (FPTP) rules tend to punish opposition parties by giving them fewer seats than their vote share might suggest. The most commonly proposed remedy has been introducing some element of proportionality, usually by adding list-based legislative seats that will compensate for the distortions of the plurality system, under a scheme known as "mixed member proportionality" (MMP).

Three recent proposals for electoral reform at the provincial level (notably for a single transferable vote scheme in British Columbia, and for MMP in Prince Edward Island and Ontario) were defeated in public referenda. After a close vote in 2005, BC promised to bring the proposal back for a second vote in 2009. New Brunswick scheduled a referendum on MMP for 2008, which was called off due to a change in government, while efforts have been made to raise the issue of electoral reform at the federal level, in Quebec, and elsewhere.[19]

One obvious question about electoral reform is the extent to which recent debates have highlighted women's participation. If public discussion is limited, or becomes bogged down in the arcane details of different voting systems, then there's little opportunity to talk about why we need change. The benefits of alternative arrangements to the quality of our democracy may in those cases become obscured, as the focus turns to precise mechanics about constructing coalition governments or ranking preference votes in multi-member districts, which—for most citizens—hold all the allure of reading an automobile manual.

To their credit, some provincial governments created citizens' assemblies (with members chosen at random from voter lists) and charged them with the task of generating a reform proposal. In Ontario in 2007, the Citizens' Assembly produced a highly readable brochure titled *One Ballot, Two Votes: A New Way to Vote in Ontario*. Written in clear language, and illustrated with helpful examples, the pamphlet recommended reducing the number of constituency seats at Queen's Park to 90 (from 107) and creating 39 at-large legislators, to be chosen from party lists in proportion to the popular vote for each party. The text argued directly that MMP would offer "stronger representation" for the people of Ontario, notably by helping to elect "more women and other citizens currently under-represented in the legislature." Voters would also know more about the entire slate of candidates fielded by each party, because they would "be able to see whether a party's list has a good balance of men and women, includes candidates from all of Ontario's regions, and reflects the diversity of Ontario's population."[20]

By identifying representation as an issue and by highlighting MMP's ability to foster a more diverse legislature plus higher voter turnout, *One Ballot* kept the focus on improving democracy. Yet the Assembly's recommendation that "a comprehensive, well-funded public education program" take place during the six months prior to the referendum did not happen. Instead, volunteer advocates on both sides of the issue tried to get people engaged. It is notable that in the run-up to the vote, opponents of the proposal generally lauded the goal of electing more women. Instead, they focused their criticisms on party lists (arguing they would increase the power of party elites), political stability (claiming it would decline under coalition governments that were dependent on the support of smaller parties), and representation (adding list members would not compensate for the loss of 17 local constituencies).[21]

Ultimately, the 2007 proposal for reforming elections in Ontario fell far short of victory. Both major provincial parties largely ignored the proposal, perhaps because it was in their interest to retain the existing system. As well, the definition of success for the new proposal was far more exacting than for winning a majority government. At least 60 percent of referendum voters across the province had to support the reform, as well as a majority of voters in at least 60 percent of the province's electoral districts. No Ontario political party since 1937 had won even 50 percent of the popular vote, meaning the referendum threshold in 2007 was far above the electoral norm that had prevailed in the province for seven decades.[22] Clearly, those who made the rules and benefited from the status quo had figured out how to dangle the prospect of change, knowing that with the threshold imposed in 2007, reform was highly unlikely.

Groups including Fair Vote Canada that pressed hard for electoral reform found it difficult to stimulate public interest in this issue, let alone to win public support for proposals that would alter the rules of the game. Yet if pro-change campaigners were able to direct the public's attention toward the consequences of getting more women and other diverse categories into politics, then perhaps the struggle would not be quite so tough. For an example of the positive effect that more women in a legislature can have, let's look at Quebec. It has reached a roughly one-third level of elected women in the National Assembly (without implementing proportional representation) and, at the same time, has created one of North America's most advanced child-care systems. There is also much to learn from Quebec about how women's organizations can pressure parties in an SMP environment to nominate female candidates in winnable seats and, from that base, how elected politicians can secure valuable policy gains to benefit society at large.[23]

Proposal 4: Contest Media Portrayals

If so much of the identifiable unease surrounding women and power flows from the communications media, then it would be absurd to focus all our energies on reforming elections or parties. Balanced portrayals in newspaper, magazine, radio, TV, and Internet coverage are crucial in order to ensure that current participants get a fair chance at being heard as authoritative speakers on matters of substance. New recruits are unlikely to be attracted to public life as long as those presently active are systematically ignored, trivialized, or dissected along various style dimensions, and then usually found wanting.

Contesting media portrayals in a formal way is extremely tricky. First of all, civil liberties in general and freedom of expression in particular are highly valued in Canada, as reflected in the text of the 1982 Charter of Rights and Freedoms. Media organizations over the years have vigorously employed these constitutional provisions in order to defend their decisions to present varied, controversial perspectives to a public audience. Lawyers for news companies often rely on a claim that readers, listeners, and viewers have the capacity to sift through disparate points of view, including those reflecting questionable judgment in the depiction of individuals and groups.

Second, struggling against biased press coverage is an inherently reactive approach. Claimants who pursue this strategy either need to accumulate a great deal of evidence that they are not being treated fairly, or else wait until a particularly egregious circumstance unfolds so that they can mount an effective challenge. Even then, there is reason to believe it's better to be proactive and perhaps celebrate balanced accounts of political women (as suggested later in this chapter), rather than to give more attention to bad practices in news organizations. Waiting until negative stories accumulate—whether in one outlet or a collection of them—is hardly an inspiring approach to democratic reform. Moreover, it can have the unintended consequence of perpetuating negative stereotypes and even elevating the profile of weak journalism.

Third, fighting media portrayals in the courts would likely prove costly on a number of levels, and may not succeed. Federal funding for the Court Challenges Program was cut by two different federal governments, those of Mulroney and Harper, and remains far from reliable even when it is in place—given the number of claimants seeking to use the same pot of money. Litigation also requires organization, meaning a lead protagonist ready and willing to take on the cause of balanced coverage. Agreeing to shoulder the burden of formal action would also be costly from the perspective of personal reputation, since elected politicians or candidates who lodged complaints might experience an even rougher ride afterwards from reporters.

Even with these constraints, there is arguably an educational benefit that would accrue from attempts to hold reporters, editors, and publishers publicly responsible for the stories and images they disseminate. Formal action could take three possible forms: a criminal court challenge, a civil court challenge, or a written complaint process. Let's examine the pros and cons of each in turn.

To proceed with legal action, a plaintiff would need to come forward with evidence that a news story, a series of stories, or some other portrayal (for example, an editorial cartoon) significantly violated Charter equality provisions. To bring the case into the realm of criminal law, litigants would need to prove the use of hateful speech. The closest parallel to gender equality litigation of this type probably involves claims by Jewish groups that a particular presentation wilfully promoted hatred against an identifiable group and was not protected by constitutional free speech provisions, as occurred in the Keegstra case.[24]

Relevant sections of the Criminal Code, however, prohibit only the expression of hatred against people who are distinguished by their colour, race, religion, ethnic origin, and, since 2004, sexual orientation. Attempts to add the category of sex to the Code's list have not been successful, even though they have been made for a number of years.[25] If harassment, intimidation, or the threat of physical force entered into the experiences of female politicians, then plaintiffs could try to claim that they were targeted as a group. In this way, gender could be "read in" to the criminal law, much as sexual orientation was introduced to Charter equality provisions via court decisions.

Documenting misogynist intentions of a criminal variety remains difficult, however. Even groups that were explicitly named in the Criminal Code have been hardpressed to make use of the hate crime sections that were added in 1970. Plaintiffs need to demonstrate that hatred was being wilfully expressed. Moreover, they confront various defences specified in the Code that, for example, permit opinions to be voiced on a religious subject if those arguments are expressed in good faith.[26] Religiously grounded claims from the social right that women should not participate in politics, for example, might well be seen as permissible under such provisions.

Given this background, women who seek redress are probably better off pursuing their cases in civil law or via self-regulatory bodies in the media industry. Either approach could be initiated by a retired politician, or by an independent organization as part of a class-action lawsuit, so that no individual who hoped to build a political career was directly linked to the case. In Canada, few retiring politicians have sought to settle scores from their public lives using any lever beyond published memoirs. This is not surprising, given that many remain fundamentally loyal to their own parties and, as well, to a larger media network in which they were immersed while in office.

Moreover, litigation by a single individual means one person bears the financial expense, stress, and risk entailed in going to court. So let's consider the possibility of class-action civil litigation, which is permissible in most Canadian provinces. This process shares the burden of legal action, by permitting people to pool their resources to fight a case if they are raising common issues across a group or class of plaintiffs.

The class-action approach has been used most often with respect to product liability claims—for example, against the tobacco industry or the makers of breast implants. Demonstrating that women candidates, elected women politicians, women party leaders, or a combined class of individuals known as female politicians were collectively damaged by unfair media coverage would establish a common issue foundation for a lawsuit. This approach would require one or more lead parties (known as representative plaintiffs) to initiate the action on behalf of the larger group.

Class-action lawsuits cannot move forward until they are certified by the court at a certification hearing. At this stage, participants need to demonstrate that they are raising shared issues, and that the class-action process is preferable to alternative channels. To meet the latter criterion, it can be helpful to demonstrate having exhausted other avenues, including the complaints processes that exist in individual media organizations as well as across communications industries in Canada.

Initiating a formal complaint about media coverage is much less onerous than going to court, but more pro-active than doing nothing at all. Lodging a complaint can serve many useful purposes. It creates the foundation for a larger class-action process, and holds the potential for stimulating meaningful reforms in media organizations that want to avoid the fallout from complaints, let alone class-action litigation. As well, by drawing attention to the portrayal of one woman or a group of women politicians, this type of complaint can raise public awareness about the ways in which reporters, columnists, editorial writers, and cartoonists present material to Canadian audiences.

Among print media outlets, individual newspapers and magazines typically have accuracy or editorial units that field complaints from the public. Press councils that more widely monitor the print sector exist in many Canadian provinces, including Alberta, Manitoba, Ontario, and Quebec. They were created during the 1970s and 1980s as a way to avoid heightened government regulation. Press councils are widely seen as a case of failed self-regulation, however, for the simple reason that industry insiders who judge their peers rarely break ranks with others in the same sector.[27]

On the electronic media side, the CBC and the larger Canadian Broadcast Standards Council post their public complaints procedures on websites, as does the Canadian Association of Internet Providers.[28] Serious breaches of standards can be taken to the federal regulatory body known as the Canadian Radio-television and Telecommunications Commission. As is the case with the print media, critics have questioned the value of these monitoring bodies because they generally draw their members from the very organizations that are under scrutiny. Lodging complaints of this type, however, seems like a necessary first step that would need to come before other actions such as individual civil litigation or a class-action lawsuit.

The Hidden Clout of Informal Strategies
Proposal 5: Movement Renewal

Who would pursue any of these formal avenues for change, whether to enhance citizen involvement, increase numbers of women candidates, reform the electoral system, or ensure fair coverage of political participants?

We need a pro-equality movement that is energetic, broadly based, and parliamentary-focused to take the lead. At the federal level and in most provinces outside Quebec, Canadians have not heard a legitimate, credible, or cohesive feminist voice for many years. The umbrella organization known as the National Action Committee on the Status of Women (NAC) has been largely invisible even to politically attentive citizens since roughly 1993, when the group came out in opposition to the Charlottetown constitutional accord. That's about 15 years before this writing, which demographers refer to as a generation.

Active women and politics groups exist in many cities, and are linked through a dynamic network of ties to Equal Voice/À voix égales, a multi-partisan group that seeks to elect more women to public office at all levels. Since 2001, Equal Voice has highlighted the stagnant or declining numbers of female city councillors, provincial legislators, and MPs across Canada. The group has consistently challenged party leaders to nominate more women candidates, and has worked hard to recruit and train potential candidates—including by launching an online campaign school known as "Getting to the Gate." Equal Voice chapters have been established in communities across Canada, and a youth wing was formed in 2005 to ensure young women are deeply involved.

As creative as Equal Voice has been in training a spotlight on the importance of electing more women—and strengthening democracy in Canada—it can't succeed by itself. Neither can the Women's Legal Education and Action Fund, known as LEAF, which is dedicated to using the terms of the Charter of Rights and Freedoms to advance women's equality. Nor can the Canadian Women's Foundation, a charitable organization that aims to improve the lives of women and girls.

Each of these groups, and others like them, lacks the visibility and influence of a national umbrella organization. Moreover, none on its own can attain the profile or clout that NAC wielded during its early years. No single organization, acting alone, can foster the climate of opinion that will ensure women take their rightful places as public participants in Canada. Nor can any one of them alone be expected to shape the policy thinking of politicians, bureaucrats, and back-room decision makers.

In a nutshell, that's why we need to imagine larger vehicles that will advance the mainstream parliamentary equality agenda of diverse women across Canada. The focus of new organizations—whether they are provincial umbrellas modeled on the Quebec Women's Federation or a federal umbrella group—would be improving the institutions of Canadian government at all levels, ensuring women are well-represented in them, and pressing for women-friendly public policies in such areas as employment, reproductive health, the environment, family law, violence, and pensions. For more than a decade, little in the way of external organized pressure has pushed provincial politicians (outside Quebec) or our federal-level political parties, notably those in the moderate middle of the spectrum, to assert core equality values or to speak publicly about the threats facing the Canadian judiciary from the social right.

New umbrella voices operating in the provinces and at the federal level would do just that. They could build on the foundations laid by suffragists and other first-wave feminists, and on the contributions of second-wave activists during the 1970s and following. These groups could take a variety of forms, either as short-term civic equality projects or longer-term coalitions that evoke the work that came before and the struggles still to be undertaken, under a name like the Canadian Organization for Democratic Advocacy, or CODA for short.

Ideally, a new Canada-wide omnibus group would attract progressive people of many ages, with diverse backgrounds and experiences. Veterans of second-wave feminism, who wonder what happened to the crucial parliamentary agenda of the Royal Commission and of NAC's early years, are an obvious source of recruits. So are young university students—including the men and women I teach—who have studied Canadian history and maintain there's still lots to be done to improve our political process and public policies.

CODA would be better off if it relied primarily on membership and foundation support, rather than on government funding. In the best case scenario, its goals, purpose, and political agenda would be clearly distinguishable from those of extraparliamentary campaigners who show no interest in institutional involvement. Activists drawn to a new umbrella organization could focus on bringing the diverse women of Canada's many cities and regions forward in the mainstream arena, thus avoiding NAC's bitter internal struggles that divided and frequently alienated pro-equality interests from one other.

Who could help to create a new umbrella group? In addition to Equal Voice, LEAF, and the Canadian Women's Foundation, each of which emerged since Charter rights came into effect in 1985, we can look to many of the same organizations that were crucial to NAC's establishment in the early 1970s. They included organizations of teachers, nurses, and women university graduates, as well as the *Fédération des femmes du Québec*, the YWCA, the National Council of Women of Canada, and associations of women executives. In every case, the groups I've listed have demonstrated sustained interest in the here-and-now of mainstream public engagement, even when that focus was far from fashionable. By forming a renewed voice for Canadians who care about the life of the polity, a new umbrella organization could place renewed emphasis on the quality of democratic citizenship in this country.

Proposal 6: Monitor the Media

A significant opportunity exists for Equal Voice, or for new equality organizations focused on improving media portrayals, to build on the work of scholars who've studied the treatment of political women in both print and electronic communications. Ongoing public scrutiny to supplement academic research could evaluate the quantity of coverage, to determine whether female politicians receive a fair share of attention, as well as the content of stories, to assess the degree to which these accounts are balanced, accurate, and offer serious versus trivialized portrayals. Organized in this way, media monitoring can carefully analyze stories about local, provincial, and federal politics.

The goal of the exercise would be to ensure greater balance in portrayals of Canadians who enter public life, using data gathered by media monitors to pursue formal sanctions of the type discussed earlier. For example, those collecting materials could choose to lodge complaints with broadcasting and press standards councils, or write letters to the editors of newspapers and magazines, or submit op-ed, opinion, and talk-back pieces that highlight their concerns and publicize the results of their monitoring work.

More importantly, an organization devoted to media scrutiny could generate positive incentives for reporters and news companies. Above all, meaningful awards ceremonies in communities across the country can recognize best practices in radio, television, print, and Internet news. They might recognize, for instance, exceptionally sensitive, in-depth coverage by reporters, columnists, or editorial writers. By focusing on the positive, they'd celebrate the efforts of both individuals and news organizations to resist the usual stereotypes, and to overturn rather than reinforce the *women plus power equals discomfort* equation.

The question of how political women are treated in media stories might also figure in the curriculum of journalism schools. A group based in Toronto during the 1990s, known as MediaWatch, developed pedagogical materials designed for use in just such courses.[29] More recently, the Ryerson University School of Journalism sponsored a Diversity Watch program, to scrutinize the numbers of women and ethno-cultural minorities working in Canadian newsrooms.[30] Media watch organizations that analyze the portrayal of women and girls have been created in many other countries, including Jamaica and South Africa, and offer intriguing models for online as well as classroom education activities.[31]

Informal scrutiny of news stories can also happen outside organizations and classrooms. As individuals, we can each challenge media constructions of women in public life by asking tough questions about the ways in which proposals for reform—including changes to the electoral system, the introduction of quotas for candidates, and other ideas—are treated in the media. This type of action relies on individual acts of courage that directly challenge the *discomfort equation*. We can ask directly whether the reforms under consideration are likely to benefit or disadvantage women. Do reporters covering the story address all sides of a new idea? Or does their framing of the proposal constitute an implicit vote of confidence in the status quo?

Reflecting on her own experiences in public life, and her close reading of the work of Virginia Valian, Kim Campbell recommended precisely this type of strategy. Writing in 2006, she argued: "I have come to believe that the only way to open up opportunities for women is for all of us to become 'schema busters' through understanding why barriers still exist for women even in the face of real accomplishment and by making visible all those women who defy the stereotypes. This means nothing less than changing the landscape from which people derive their ideas of what are normal gender roles."[32]

One way to begin this type of scrutiny is by conducting random thought-check experiments. The next time you're watching, reading, or listening to the media that surround us, ask yourself what the alternatives might look or sound like. How would a story about a woman party leader or a local mayor more accurately present the qualities she brings to public life? What perspectives could be brought to the table if women journalists regularly posed more of the questions at party leaders' debates? Are election night commentators probing the sorts of concerns you'd like to see addressed?

What's most exciting is that informal scrutiny of what goes on in press coverage can engage lots of younger, media-savvy Canadians in our political process. It can pose hard questions about who gets portrayed, in what ways, and by whom in the communications industry. And above all, activities of this sort can breathe life into the old saying, "Don't get angry, get even." Since the decline of NAC, MediaWatch, and other organizations, reporters in Canada have enjoyed a relatively free ride when it comes to framing their coverage of women in politics. It's time to say "enough is enough," and use freedom of expression protections as an invitation to open our own mouths—rather than to have that protection used exclusively by the usual purveyors of news and public commentary.

Proposal 7: Probe Anti-Feminism

The first two informal steps recommended in this chapter entailed reinvigorating a parliamentary-focused women's movement and monitoring media coverage in a serious way. Taken together, they provide an essential foundation for confronting the looming but never silent elephant in the room, namely organized anti-feminism. Precisely whom does REAL Women represent? How many members pay annual dues? Are REAL Women's leaders elected by the group's general membership? Who decides about issue priorities? What sources of funding support the organization, besides federal government grants?

Unfortunately, Canadian media outlets have not posed these crucial questions. Many of them routinely quote Gwen Landolt, a lawyer who has spoken on behalf of REAL Women since the 1980s and who holds the title of national vice-president. Landolt also serves as a director of the Canadian Justice Review Board (CJRB), a group of conservative anti–Charter of Rights and Freedoms activists who have been highly critical of both the Court Challenges Program and of progressive decisions by Canadian courts. Other CJRB directors include Robert Martin, a law professor at the University of Western Ontario who was appointed by the Harper Conservatives in January 2007 to the Federal Judicial Advisory Committee for Ontario.[33]

The same energy that reporters directed toward dissecting Kim Campbell's leadership style or, more recently, Belinda Stronach's wardrobe could have been better directed toward probing the underpinnings of organized anti-feminism in Canada. It doesn't matter whether the cause of this oversight is sloppiness, laziness, or implicit agreement with the goals of REAL Women—the point is that journalists need to step up to the plate and start interrogating their interlocutors. Trade union leaders state clearly for whom they speak. So do bank presidents, ambassadors from other countries, and mayors of cities. It's about time that Gwen Landolt and others who are involved in Canada's top anti-feminist group were asked to do the same, and state precisely whom they represent.

One of the reasons we know so little about REAL Women is that the group has blocked scholarly access for close to 20 years. To my knowledge, no unaffiliated graduate student or faculty member from a Canadian university has gained entrance to a meeting or conference sponsored by REAL Women during the decades that research access has been sought. Unlike NAC, which held annual general meetings that were full of reporters and academics, and which opened group archives to public study, REAL Women has been very much a closed shop since it burst onto the scene in the 1980s.

What's all the secrecy about? I suspect that like other far right organizations, REAL Women prefers to keep its entrails well hidden because they would frighten most Canadians. The group operates in the same realm as other hard-right interests, including many evangelical and funda-mentalist religious sects, radical anti-abortion campaigners, pro-gun activists, and Charter critics (many of whom are more accurately described as "Charter-phobes"). Taken together, these interests oppose core views that remain popular among the general public—whether they involve the value of separation of church and state in Canada, a woman's right to choose, the need to limit firearms in cities, or the importance of having courts uphold the provisions of the Charter of Rights and Freedoms.

Obviously, REAL Women and other groups like it have every right to try to change public opinion. They simply need to be drawn out of the shadows so we know who they represent, where they get their funding, and what qualifies their leaders to turn public policies in directions that are inconsistent with what most Canadians want. If we had a strong, parliamentary-focused, pro-equality movement in Canada, and if that movement inspired women as well as men to press the media to do their jobs, then we'd all know a lot more about each of these questions. As well, a great deal more analytic light would shine on the entire Canadian social right—not just organized anti-feminism.

Proposal 8: Get Involved in Politics

There are limits to what standing on the sidelines can accomplish. Good people need to jump in with both feet to the school boards, city councils, political parties, and cross-party groups that make change happen in our communities. We need to engage our children early on, by taking them with us to vote and by ensuring they understand how our political system works and what could be improved in public life.

It's not difficult to start this process. Find an issue that you care about, and pursue your concerns wherever they lead—whether it's toward the mayor's office, 24 Sussex Drive in Ottawa, or perhaps an organization like Equal Voice that works to keep women's participation in the public eye. Whichever vehicle or level of government you choose, you're sure to meet interesting people who share common values, and together you can generate a sense of excitement about the opportunities that exist to make democracy better.

Small steps can make a big difference. A recent study by two political scientists, Christine Cheng and Margit Tavits, showed that the presence of female constituency association presidents in Canada significantly increased the probability that local parties would nominate women candidates.[34] This finding makes sense in intuitive terms, given that constituency association leaders often aim toward candidacy themselves. Women riding presidents could be very open to female nominees, and anxious to foster positive views of them, because such perspectives can assist their own upward mobility. In short, the Cheng and Tavits study reminds us not to discount the role of local party work.

Equal Voice is a lively, buoyant organization that has attracted the support of many committed women and men across Canada. Building on the foundations established by Women for Political Action in the 1970s, and by the Committee for '94 and other groups during the 1980s and following, Equal Voice set its sights on raising the numbers of women who hold office at all levels. The organization skilfully uses the power of public suasion to convince party leaders to nominate more female candidates.

These actions get results. In the run-up to the fall 2007 Ontario provincial election, for example, Equal Voice pressed party leaders of all stripes to do their part to get the numbers of women elected to the legislature back on the upswing from the decline that occurred during the Mike Harris years in the mid-1990s and following. This campaign was effective: the three major parties ran more women in 2007 than in 2003, and the numbers of female MPPs surpassed the previous record to reach 30 of 107, or 28 percent.

Since public life is about discourse as well as action, the options before us extend well beyond the boundaries of running for office or joining Equal Voice. It's important to talk about the importance of enhancing citizen engagement in Canadian politics with your friends, neighbours, and family members—especially if they are young and impressionable. Children who grow up hearing about public life around the kitchen table tend to know the issues, understand their responsibility to get involved, and feel effective once they do engage in the political arena.

It's crucial to share your experiences and knowledge with people of all ages, so we all learn from each other. If you're in a book club or are thinking of starting one, encourage the readers around you to devote some time to learning about the political history of women in Canada. Local public libraries carry fascinating biographies of Agnes Macphail, Belinda Stronach, Kim Campbell, and many others. Engaging memoirs that document the challenges of public life have been written by many provincial and federal politicians, including Rosemary Brown, Sharon Carstairs, Thérèse Casgrain, Kim Campbell, Audrey McLaughlin, Lise Payette, Sheila Copps, and Judy LaMarsh. If your preference is fiction, bear in mind that LaMarsh also wrote two racy novels, which have been widely interpreted as thinly disguised accounts of the private and public lives of politicians in Ottawa.

Should you wish to delve into the lives of political women outside Canada, then by all means wade into the voluminous literatures about Hillary Clinton, Indira Gandhi, Golda Meir, Benazir Bhutto, Gro Harlem Brundtland (former prime minister of Norway), Mary Robinson (former president of Ireland), Ellen Johnson-Sirleaf (president of Liberia), and many others. With a grant from the United Nations, the Inter-Parliamentary

Union has constructed a comprehensive bibliography about women and politics across the continents. The database covers not just popular but also academic titles, and is easy to use.[35]

Among the most important things we as individuals can contribute to political talk and action is to embrace multiple styles of public leadership for women as well as men, so we get out from under traditional stereotypes. In our conversations with others, we can refuse to underestimate women's potential to contribute to politics, and can reject notions that women in public life must be perfect. These are meaningful, doable acts that—if they happen often enough—can put a big red X across the *women plus power equals discomfort* equation.

Notes

1. See http://www.idea.int/vt/compulsory_voting.cfm, consulted 3 October 2007.
2. See http://www.idea.int/publications/voter_turnout_weurope/upload/chapter%203.pdf, consulted 3 October 2007.
3. See http://www.idea.int/vt/survey/voter_turnout_pop2.cfm, consulted 3 October 2007.
4. Elections Ontario reported the 2007 Ontario election turnout was 52.7 percent of voters on the voters' list.
5. See http://www.irpp.org/wp/archive/wp2006-03.pdf, and http://www.cbc.ca/canada/toronto/story/2006/11/14/turnout-toronto.html?ref=rss, consulted 3 October 2007. The latter account reports turnout in Toronto appeared to rise from 38 percent in 2003 to 41% in 2006 because about 250,000 names (or about 16% of the people on the voters' list) were deleted in 2006 since their citizenship was not confirmed.
6. See http://www.canada.com/montrealgazette/news/story.html?id=90e935e2-afef-4581-bb94-1b3b28549828&k=3352, consulted 3 October 2007.

7. See http://vancouver.ca/ctyclerk/elections/voter_turnout.
   htm, consulted 3 October 2007.
8. Papavero found no evidence in Europe of contagion from left
   party quotas to other parts of the spectrum. See Licia Papavero,
   "Competing for Women: Female Legislative Recruitment in
   Italy and Spain," paper presented at American Political
   Science Association meetings, Chicago, September 2007.
9. In 1989, the party's Ontario wing adopted guidelines that said
   50 percent of all provincial constituencies should field female
   candidates, as should 60% of winnable or priority seats. The
   guidelines also stipulated that constituencies without an
   NDP incumbent could not hold a nomination meeting until
   at least one candidate was nominated from a "specific target
   group" (which included women, visible minorities, disabled
   and aboriginal people).
10. See http://canada.justice.gc.ca/en/ps/const/loireg/p1t1-1.
    html, consulted 4 October 2007.
11. See http://en.wikipedia.org/wiki/British_North_America_
    Act, consulted 4 October 2007.
12. See Sujit Choudhry and Michael Pal, "Is Every Ballot Equal?
    Visible Minority Vote Dilution," *IRPP Choices* 13: 1 (2007),
    1–30.
13. See http://www.ksg.harvard.edu/wappp/research/working/
    pippa_norris.pdf, consulted 4 October 2007.
14. Reforms introduced in 2002 set up a 50/50 rule, and specified
    placements for women and men on the top of party lists. See
    http://www.quotaproject.org/displayCountry.cfm?CountryC
    ode=BE, consulted 4 October 2007.
15. See http://www.elections.ca/eca/eim/article_search/article.
    asp?id=127&lang=e&frmPageSize=&textonly=false,
    consulted 4 October 2007.
16. See, for example, http://www.elections.on.ca/NR/rdonlyres/
    27651D3C-51CB-4081-9A62-8F0596121629/0/EFA_Report_
    English_Final_Web_OCt_05.pdf, consulted 4 October 2007;
    http://www.elections.sk.ca/taxcredit.php, consulted 5 Oct-
    ober 2007; http://www.gnb.ca/legis/OSPF-BCFP/PDF/2003
    AnnualReport.pdf, consulted 5 October 2007.

17. Candidate quotas at the local and municipal level could only work if there were visible parties operating in a given jurisdiction. In a number of major Canadian cities including Montreal and Vancouver, local parties are known to voters, while in others like Toronto, only the NDP identifies itself in city elections.

18. See http://www.ksg.harvard.edu/wappp/research/working/pippa_norris.pdf, page 3, consulted 5 October 2007. Norris's argument is confirmed with reference to Canada in Dennis Pilon, *The Politics of Voting: Reforming Canada's Electoral System* (Toronto: Emond Montgomery, 2007), 41–42, 58–61.

19. See http://www.sfu.ca/~aheard/elections/reform.html, consulted 5 October 2007.

20. Ontario Citizens' Assembly on Electoral Reform, *One Ballot, Two Votes: A New Way to Vote in Ontario* (Toronto: Queen's Printer for Ontario, 2007), 3, 9.

21. According to a detailed survey on this subject, Ontario voters were generally satisfied with the existing electoral system, but liked the MMP proposal increasingly as they learned more about it. Voters knew little about the proposal, however, or its origins in a citizens' assembly, and tended not to like either a larger legislature or the control parties would wield over proportional lists. See Fred Cutler and Patrick Fournier, "Why Ontarians Said No to MMP," *The Globe and Mail* (25 October 2007), A21.

22. See http://www.fairvotecanada.org/files/FVOflyer-nov1605.pdf, consulted 8 October 2007.

23. See Manon Tremblay with the assistance of Stephanie Mullen, "Women in the Quebec National Assembly: Why So Many?" in Sylvia Bashevkin, ed., *Opening Doors Wider: Women's Political Engagement in Canada* (Vancouver: UBC Press, 2009), 51–69.

24. See http://en.wikipedia.org/wiki/R._v._Keegstra, consulted 8 October 2007.

25. See http://www.fradical.com/The_Public_Has_a_Right_to_be_Safe.pdf, consulted 8 October 2007.

26. See http://www.parl.gc.ca/information/library/PRBpubs/
    856-e.htm, consulted 9 October 2007.
27. See http://www.parl.gc.ca/Infoparl/english/issue.htm?param
    =84&art=261, consulted 8 October 2007.
28. See http://www.media-awareness.ca/english/resources/codes
    _guidelines/television/cbc/cbc_journalistic_code.cfm; http://
    www.cbsc.ca/english/main/home.htm; and http:// www.
    media-awareness.ca/english/resources/codes_guidelines/
    internet/caip._code_of_conduct.cfm, consulted 8 October
    2007.
29. See http://www.cfc-efc.ca/docs/vanif/00000139.htm; and
    http://www.sfu.ca/cmns/faculty/murray_c/assets/Media
    Watch.pdf, consulted 10 October 2007.
30. See http://www.diversitywatch.ryerson.ca/home_miller_2004
    report.htm, consulted 10 October 2007.
31. See http://www.diversitywatch.ryerson.ca/home_miller_ 2004
    report.htm; and http://www.womensmediawatch.org.za/
    wmw/whatwedo.html; consulted 10 October 2007.
32. Kim Campbell, "Three for Thought: What You Need to Know
    about ... Women on Top," *The Globe and Mail* (28 January
    2006), D15.
33. See http://www.canadianjusticereviewboard.ca/NEWSROOM.
    HTM, consulted 11 October 2007.
34. Christine Cheng and Margit Tavits, "Gatekeepers and Money:
    What Affects Canadian Women's Electoral Success?" paper
    presented at American Political Science Association meetings,
    Chicago, September 2007.
35. See http://www.ipu.org/bdf-e/BDfsearch.asp, consulted 12
    October 2007.

Index

9 780195 431704